India as Kingmaker

India as Kingmaker

Status Quo or Revisionist Power

**Michael O. Slobodchikoff and
Aakriti A. Tandon**

University of Michigan Press
Ann Arbor

For questions or permissions, please contact um.press.perms@umich.edu

Published in the United States of America by the
University of Michigan Press
Printed and bound by CPI Group (UK) Ltd, Croydon, CR0 4YY

First published December 2022

A CIP catalog record for this book is available from the British Library.

Library of Congress Cataloging-in-Publication Data

Names: Slobodchikoff, Michael O., author. | Tandon, Aakriti A., author. |
   Michigan Publishing (University of Michigan), publisher.
Title: India as kingmaker : status quo or revisionist power / Michael O. Slobodchikoff and
   Aakriti A. Tandon.
Description: Ann Arbor : University of Michigan Press, 2022. | Includes bibliographical
   references (pages 153–161) and index.
Identifiers: LCCN 2022024361 (print) | LCCN 2022024362 (ebook) |
   ISBN 9780472075669 (hardcover) | ISBN 9780472055661 (paperback) |
   ISBN 9780472220755 (ebook)
Subjects: LCSH: India—Foreign relations—21st century. | Geopolitics—
   India. | Neutrality—India. | Balance of power. | BISAC: POLITICAL SCIENCE /
   International Relations / Diplomacy | POLITICAL SCIENCE / Security (National &
   International)
Classification: LCC DS449 .S59   2022 (print) | LCC DS449 (ebook) |
   DDC 327.54—dc23/eng/20220629
LC record available at https://lccn.loc.gov/2022024361
LC ebook record available at https://lccn.loc.gov/2022024362

Cover images courtesy Shutterstock.com / T. Lesia; and Shutterstock.com / PO11

To our children, Nicholas, Ayaansh, and Aashna.
May you all grow up to see a time that is less prone
to conflict than the current one.

Contents

List of Tables   ix

List of Figures   xi

Acknowledgments   xiii

Part 1. India's Place in the Global Order

1 • India as a Kingmaker   3

2 • The Challenge to the Global Order   11

3 • Treaty Networks and Determining State Preferences
for the Global Order   36

Part 2. India's Relationship with Status Quo Powers

4 • India-US Relations   65

5 • Indo-European Relations   82

6 • Indo-Japanese Relations   99

Part 3. India's Relationship with Revisionist Powers

7 • Indo-Russian Relations   113

8 • Indo-Chinese Relations   128

9 • India's Place in the World Order:
   Revisionist or Status Quo Power?   140

   References   153

   Index   163

Digital materials related to this title can be found on
the Fulcrum platform via the following citable URL:
https://doi.org/10.3998/mpub.12330581

Tables

1 Categories of Great Powers   22
2 Status Quo vs. Revisionist Powers   37
3 Institutionalized Cooperation Scores   50
4 Cooperative Relationship Scores   51
5 Status Quo vs. Revisionist Powers   58
6 Indo-US Bilateral Treaties   74
7 Lodestone Treaties between India and the US   75
8 Level of Institutionalization in the Indo-US Relationship   79
9 India-EU Cooperation   88
10 India-UK Cooperation   91
11 India-France Cooperation   94
12 India-Germany Cooperation   97
13 India-European Powers Cooperation   97
14 India-Japan Cooperation   104
15 India-Japan Cooperation Scores   106
16 India-Russia Cooperation   121
17 India-Russia Cooperation Scores   122
18 India-Russia Lodestone Treaties   122
19 India-China Cooperation   136
20 India-China Lodestone Treaties   137
21 Cooperation Scores between India and Great Powers   146
22 Cooperation Scores between India and Status Quo Powers   147
23 Cooperation Scores between India and Revisionist Powers   148
24 Categorization of Status Quo vs. Revisionist Powers   149

Figures

1	International Order	14
2	Bipolar International Order	17
3	Global and Regional Hierarchical Order	18
4	Treaty Nesting	48
5	Treaty Network	48
6	India–South Africa Treaty Network	49
7	India-EU Treaty Network	49
8	Indo-US Treaty Network	76
9	Indo-EU Treaty Network	87
10	Indo-UK Treaty Network	89
11	Indo-France Treaty Network	94
12	Indo-Germany Treaty Network	95
13	Indo-Japanese Treaty Network	105
14	Indo-Russia Treaty Network	122
15	Indo-China Treaty Network	156

Acknowledgments

Writing a book is a true labor. Writing a book during a pandemic is close to impossible. While all of our lives have been facing uncertainty and upheaval, we fully recognize that it wouldn't have been possible to complete this task without help from many different people. To our spouses, Tatyana and Anuj, we are eternally thankful. They not only provide support in terms of allowing us to work on this project, but they are sounding boards for our ideas, and while they might be rolling their eyes having heard the details of this project so many times, we are truly thankful for each of you.

For their eternal and selfless love and support we thank our parents and sisters, who continue to shower us with positive feedback whether near or far. We are also grateful to our respective institutions, Troy University and Daemen College, for providing us with support that helped to bring this work to fruition.

We are also very thankful for the work of the editorial staff at the University of Michigan Press. Thank you to Elizabeth Demers and Haley Winkle for all of their support and willingness to help this project along. Thank you to the anonymous reviewers for all of your comments that have made this book much better. Also, a special thank you to the Executive Board of the University of Michigan Press. All of your questions and the dialogue that ensued helped clarify this book and strengthened the arguments within.

Several students helped to make this project a reality. Thank you to Billy Hines, Alicia Rodriguez-Castillo, Christian Knight, Zachary Greene, Kenny Luker, and Leandro Guimaroes Froes for all of your help in coding treaties and helping to research these treaties.

Finally, we would like to thank the Ministry of External Affairs of India for maintaining the full texts of all of their treaties and keeping this list accessible and transparent. The ability to analyze each of the treaties and determine the relationship between the treaties was invaluable to this project. We hope that all states move to this model of transparency in terms of reporting the texts of all of their treaties and agreements.

Part 1 • India's Place in the Global Order

1 • India as a Kingmaker

The presence of global anarchy is fundamental to international relations. The absence of a global government to ensure set rules and behaviors creates uncertainty in the relationship between states. However, that does not mean that global anarchy is static. Great powers are able to establish and enforce rules of interaction among states within the space in which they are able to project their power. A hegemonic power that is able to project its power globally can create a global order and the rules of interaction within that order. Following World War II, the United States became a superpower and created a liberal economic order and rules-based regime. Similarly, the Soviet Union created its own order and established rules to be followed within its sphere of influence. This is a classic bipolar system, where each superpower has control over a specific region of the globe and has created an order and rules to follow for that region. Hegemonic stability theory argues that there is less uncertainty and less violence between states where there is one hegemonic power that establishes a global order. Following the end of the Cold War, the United States became a unipolar power, and the liberal order that it had established following World War II was expanded globally. States that were once a part of the Soviet bloc now followed the global order established by the United States.

Not all states, however, are happy with the global order established by the hegemon. States that are dissatisfied with the global order may gather enough power to challenge the hegemonic state and thus the global order. These revisionist states actively want to revise the global order and challenge the global power. States that support the global order are called status quo states. In other words, they are happy with the current global order and do not wish to change or revise the current global order as they may stand to benefit from the status quo.

Power transition theory posits that when a revisionist state has amassed enough power to challenge the hegemonic state, then conflict will ensue. The reason for this is that the global hegemon does not want to relinquish control of the world order, and the revisionist state is eager to create an alternative world order. According to power transition theory, this is when we are likely to see massive conflict between states such as world wars. For example, one of the common explanations of World War I and World War II has to do with the fact that Great Britain was the global hegemon, and Germany was a revisionist power. As a rising Germany amassed enough power to challenge the global order, it did so by invoking conflict against Great Britain in World War I and World War II. However, Germany was not powerful enough to defeat the global order established by Great Britain. While emerging victorious, Great Britain was severely weakened during the world wars and was unable to continue maintaining the global order following World War II. The United States quickly stepped into the vacuum and created the liberal global order.

Following the end of the Cold War, the United States expanded the liberal order in the absence of any challengers. However, over time, states became dissatisfied with the liberal order and more specifically with the rules established by the United States. Specifically, over time, China and Russia became increasingly dissatisfied with the liberal global order. According to power transition theory, in addition to being dissatisfied, revisionist states must also have enough power to challenge the current hegemon. The rise of China's power, and the alignment of Russia's and China's positions against the United States, is challenging the current global order. Great powers in the global system must now make their preferences known. Are the great powers in favor of revising the current global order, in other words, in becoming revisionist powers, or are they in favor of maintaining the current global order, in other words, in remaining status quo powers? Many of the great powers have already aligned themselves accordingly. For example, Great Britain, France, and Germany have aligned themselves with the current global order. They are classic status quo powers. On the other side, Russia and China are aligned and are revisionist powers. One of the great powers that is an enigma is India. India can play a crucial role in determining the direction of the global order. Will India be a status quo power and thus support the United States in maintaining the current global order, or will India be a revisionist power and support China's and Russia's attempts to revise the current global order? Officially, India has declared that it is a nonaligned power. This means that India has declined to form formal alliances with either the United States or Russia. Also, India has chosen to maintain close ties with both the

United States and Russia. Given India's rising power and status in the international system, it is in the position to become a kingmaker. If the United States wants to retain the current global order, it must convince India to support the current order. If China and Russia wish to effectively challenge the global order, they must convince India to support the revisionist position. In this book, we examine India's place in the global order and determine India's preferences as to whether it is more likely to support the current order or more likely to support the revisionist powers. In other words, we determine whether India is a status quo or revisionist power. India's nonaligned status makes this a difficult, albeit interesting task. We now turn to a discussion of India's nonaligned status.

Nonalignment

Independent India's first prime minister, Pandit Jawaharlal Nehru, was the architect of modern India. As India grappled with its newfound role and responsibilities as a sovereign state, he exercised disproportionate influence on many aspects of policy making, of which foreign policy was one prominent area. Nascent India's foreign policy was largely shaped by Nehru and his ideals and ideology. Nehru was considered to be an idealist and an international statesman and he believed in India's manifest destiny to join the group of great powers. Working to that end, he intentionally shaped India's foreign policy to be unique and worth emulating by other developing states.

By the time India was coming into its own as a newly independent country, the Cold War had begun between the United States and the Soviet Union. Nehru consciously fabricated an approach based on the principles of nonalignment that would prevent India from becoming depending on either the First World (capitalist democratic) or Second World (socialist autocratic) states. While India had much in common with the democratic states of the Global North, geopolitically it was within the Soviet Union's sphere of influence. This conflict probably prevented India from showing strong support for any one ideology. Also, having just completed a century long struggle to attain its independence, India's leaders did not want to jeopardize its independence by creating formal linkages with any great power. As a result, unlike several former colonies in Africa that continue to have military ties with France, India steadfastly avoided covert and overt efforts by the United Kingdom to pursue formal military ties with its former colonial ruler.

As a newly independent country, India was undergoing growing pains; it was attempting to shape its political economy with the twin goals of achieving economic development and the eradication of social problems. Nehru believed that it was in India's best interest to maintain friendly relations with all the major powers; there was much to gain in terms of foreign aid by playing the neutrality card. As long as India remained genuinely neutral, it would not be considered a threat by any one side. On the contrary, because of its size and strategic position, both the United States and the Soviet Union would attempt to woo India by offering generous foreign aid, technology transfers, and so forth, which would aid in India's much-needed industrial development.

It was Nehru's strong desire to refrain from becoming entangled in great power conflict as well as his efforts at internal diplomacy that gave birth to the Non-Aligned Movement. Nehru, along with the leaders of Egypt and other Third World (nonaligned, developing) countries, together formed the Non-Aligned Movement.

The Non-Aligned Movement provided India with a platform to relay its message to the world. It also provided India with an opportunity to practice its leadership skills and portray its great power aspirations to the international community. While India had good intentions and used righteous language to reprimand major power states when they committed human rights abuses or neglected their global social responsibilities, it was criticized for not always living up to these ideals itself, both domestically and in its interactions with neighboring states in South Asia.

The Non-Aligned Movement's Lingering Legacy

While the Non-Aligned Movement eventually lost its fervor and rationale for existence, Nehruvian idealism and nonalignment continued to inform Indian foreign policy. The country is only now witnessing the first generation of scholars, academics, and politicians who are far enough removed from Nehru's era to question the value of nonalignment in India's foreign policy and are willing to break with this approach and undertake a new guiding philosophy.

Nehru, as India's first prime minister and external affairs minister, carefully controlled the creation and delivery of foreign policy. Nehru's principles of idealistic internationalism, self-reliance, nonalignment, *swadeshi* ('of one's own country,' i.e. made in India), and nondogmatic socialism were the underlying basis on which India's foreign policy was created (Ogden 2014).

The process of foreign policy formulation in India remains ad hoc and opaque, consisting of the Prime Minister's Office and a close group of trusted advisors. Thus, individual leaders continue to wield a significant amount of influence vis-à-vis defining the country's national interests and the direction of its foreign policy. This is not to say that there hasn't been continuity in preserving foreign policy principles with the regular change in leadership that the democratic process brings approximately every five years. However, this continuity is the result of chance rather than careful planning. It is partly because the Indian National Congress party continued to dominate the Indian electorate and stay in power for the first 50 years of India's independence. The first non-Congress-led government came to power in 1998. Congress's near domination of the Indian electorate and election process ensured continuity, rather than change, as the norm in the foreign policy creation circles.

Atal Bhiari Bajpayee (from the Bharatiya Janata Party, or BJP) was the first prime minister from outside the Indian National Congress to serve a full five-year term. His administration brought fresh insight, infused new vigor, and provided new direction to India's trajectory. It was during the BJP's tenure that India successfully tested the nuclear bomb and joined an elite group of states by becoming a nuclear power. India was an unwelcome member to this closed group of nuclear weapons states, but India remained resolute in defying other major powers and insisted that its territorial rivalry with Pakistan over the issue of Kashmir as well as the nuclear status of neighboring China, which had defeated India in an interstate war in 1962, justified India's quest for nuclear deterrence. It is these external threats and their influence on India's security policy that will be the prime subject of the next chapter.

Politicians, bureaucrats, and some scholars and members of the media continue to play lip service to nonalignment as the ideology guiding India's interactions with other states in the international system, specifically the major powers. However, nonalignment is fast receding as a foreign policy principle in India. Nehruvian idealism has been replaced by realpolitik thinking among the top brass of the country's administrators. Today, India continues to adhere to certain Nehruvian ideals such as a preference for multipolarity, equality for all states irrespective of the size of their economy and military, respect for state sovereignty as well as human rights, and the utility of international institutions in helping to appease problems of trust and coordination that are inherent in international relations. However, India and its leaders are increasingly cognizant of the role of material capabilities and the preponderance of power politics and they are willing participants in a system where inequality is rampant, in bilateral interactions as well as in multilateral institutions. In spite of the fact that India has such an interest in international relations, India is hampered by its relations with the states located in its region. We now turn to a discussion of India's place as a regional power.

India as a Regional Power

India is the most powerful of the states in South Asia. While many of the states in the region struggle with economic growth, India has witnessed massive economic growth in the last two decades. Along with economic growth, the size of India's population has also exploded. However, India has fragile and tense relations with the other states in the region. In fact, India has many territorial conflicts with neighboring states. The most well-known rivalry in the region is between India and Pakistan. It is between two nuclear states that often have militarized disputes in Kashmir, a contested border region between India and Pakistan. Both India and Pakistan lay claim to Kashmir, and often hostilities between both countries erupt into military conflict. This territorial conflict has led to two major wars between India and Pakistan in 1947 and 1965, with a limited war breaking out in 1999. In February 2019, conflict again broke out between India and Pakistan when Indian forces came under attack in Kashmir, killing several troops. India responded by aerial bombing a Pakistani base. Pakistan shot down an Indian aircraft and even captured an Indian pilot. While tensions continued to escalate, India sent more paramilitary forces into Kashmir. While the situation did not devolve into full-scale war, the situation and border conflict remain unresolved and could devolve into war should conflict break out again.

The conflict between India and Pakistan is not the only major border conflict affecting India. India and China also have a contested border region between the two states. In 1962, both sides fought a war over the contested region, resulting in India's humiliating defeat. Since 1962, tensions have been simmering between the two states, threatening to escalate into a larger conflict. In 2020, tensions escalated into armed confrontation with both India and China accusing each others' militaries of shooting at each other. While an agreement was struck in 1999, where both sides agreed not to use guns or explosives in the contested area, nevertheless armed conflict broke out in 2020, resulting in casualties for both sides. Tensions continue to boil over the contested territory, yet both sides try to keep a full military conflict from erupting. Both sides trade with each other, and China is one of India's largest trading partners, meaning that the economy of both states would suffer should a war break out. Despite their cooperation in trade, both India and China remain wary of each other. For example, when Russia wanted to invite India to join the Shanghai Cooperation Organization, China only agreed to allow India to become a member if Pakistan were also allowed membership, ensuring a type of power balancing within the organization.

Despite India's border conflicts, India remains committed to having relationships with other states in the region as well as globally. India is not only committed to bilateral relations with other states but also to being involved in multilateral institutions. One example of this is the Free and Open Indo-Pacific Strategy. This is a strategy begun by Japan as a method of providing an alternative to China's Belt and Road Initiative and to counter China's influence in the region. Four states, known as the "Quad" (the United States, Japan, India, and Australia) have come together to discuss cooperation and develop regional infrastructure projects.

Despite being involved in the Quad process and the Free and Open Indo-Pacific Strategy, India remains reluctant to fully embrace it, knowing that doing so would alienate China. Thus, India is left to tread the line between cooperation with China, balancing China's regional power, and cooperating with the current global hegemon and status quo powers.

India is an important player in the quest for creating a new global order for the 21st century. China recognizes the importance of India's power and status. If China can convince India to become a full revisionist power, then the revisionist powers will be successful in wresting control of the global order. The United States, in return, understands India's importance in maintaining the current global order and retaining the status quo. In this way, India is truly a kingmaker. If India chooses to become a revisionist power, the global order will witness change. Whereas, if India chooses to be a status quo power, China's bid to challenge the current global order would be unsuccessful. In this book, we examine India's bilateral relations with the major status quo and revisionist powers to determine where India's preferences lie in determining the future of the global order.

This book is separated into three sections. Part 1 discusses India's place in the global order. Part 2 discusses India's relations with the status quo states, while part 3 discusses India's relations with revisionist powers. In chapter 2, we delve into the concepts of world order and how world order is created. We examine the current world order established by the United States following World War II, and categorize global powers as either status quo or revisionist. In chapter 3, we describe the methodology that we use to determine India's preferences toward the global order. We examine India's bilateral treaties with status quo and revisionist states as an indicator of the country' preference toward the global order.

Part 2 of the book is an analysis of India's relationships with the great status quo powers. Thus, chapter 4 examines the relationship between the United States and India. While the United States has stated that it has made a pivot to Asia and that its relationship with India is a priority, we examine the bilateral relationship to determine the accuracy of this view.

India has a special relationship with the United Kingdom, one of the biggest allies of the United States, and one of the strongest proponents of the liberal order. Because of the United Kingdom's colonial past in India, with chapter 5 we examine their bilateral relationship to determine the level of cooperation between those two states and whether or not their relationship indicates support for the liberal order. The European Union is also a strong ally and proponent of the liberal order. Two of the major powers within the European Union are France and Germany. Therefore, in addition to examining India's relationship with the UK, chapter 5 focuses on the bilateral relationships between India and France and India and Germany as well as India's relationship with the EU.

In chapter 6 we turn to examine status quo states in Asia. Specifically, we focus on India's relationship with Japan. Japan is a longtime ally of the United States and a supporter of the liberal order, and has been increasingly concerned with the rise of China's power in the region. India's relationship with Japan will indicate its openness to maintaining the liberal order.

In part 3, we begin to examine India's relationships with revisionist powers. Thus, in chapter 7 we focus on its relationship with Russia. Given that India had close ties with the Soviet Union, it is important to examine its ties with Russia following the collapse of the Soviet Union to see if India's preference is for revising the liberal order. In chapter 8 we examine India's relationship with China. This could be more of a problematic relationship as India and China have had border disputes and a rivalry. However, if India is truly a revisionist state, it will have a cooperative relationship with China. Finally, in chapter 9, we determine India's preference toward the liberal order. We offer not only a determination of India's preference but also provide policy recommendations for how to proceed in bilateral relationships with India for both the status quo and revisionist states.

2 • The Challenge to the Global Order

The concept of hierarchical power distribution in the global order has long been a central component of international relations. Initially, global order was seen as being a reflection of order created by states within their own geographical boundaries. For example, Huntington ([1968] 2006) argues that order is the most important factor for a state's survival. What he means by order is a regime's ability to control and maintain stability within its geographical borders. He states that the type of government is not as important as internal order. Governments or regimes create institutions, which establish order and stability. Rapid social change in societies, coupled with the inability of institutions to meet the new demands of society, leads to a lack of order and stability. While order and stability seem to be synonymous for Huntington, it is important to note several important aspects of his understanding of the concept of order. Order is not a static concept. It is rather an evolving concept that depends upon the interaction between society on the one hand and institutions and rules on the other. Order creates predictability for its citizens. The rules and institutions that provide order also provide predictability and the ability for citizens to effectively operate in the system to achieve their personal goals. It should be noted that not all personal goals are alike, but rather the order that the system provides shapes the goals that individuals can have within the political system. While different regimes establish different institutional arrangements within their borders, the goal of each regime is to establish and maintain order.

While Huntington (1968) focused on the concept of intrastate order, the concept of interstate or international order is a very important topic of concern among international relations scholars. In fact, Ikenberry (2011, 22) argues that the problem of order is the central problem of international relations. More specifically, he states that the main questions in understanding the concept of order is how it is devised, how it breaks down, and how it is created. In this book, we will examine how order is created at the global level and the role of regional powers in maintaining or challenging that global order. We argue that regional powers are the lynchpins in maintaining global order as established by the hegemon. They are the ones that are responsible for helping to adhere to the rules established by the global hegemon, and must in turn not only adhere to those rules but also enforce them through their interactions with other states. Global order begins to break down when the regional great powers begin to challenge those rules, leading to a change in the hierarchical power structure among states in the global system. In the South Asia region, India is a regional great power, and is central to ensuring that the global rules are adhered to and enforced in the region. In this chapter, we will define the concept of international order, discuss how international order applies to regional power structures and regional order, and then examine the regional order in South Asia.

Conceptualizing International Order

According to hegemonic stability theory, global anarchy is part of the fundamental nature of the global system. There is no world government, and thus states must provide for their own security. However, theorists believe that anarchy is not static. Instead, they argue that if a state is able to become a hegemonic power, that state will be able to establish rules by which the rest of the states in the global system must abide. The hegemon can enforce the rules either through the use of overwhelming force or through ostracization by not allowing states that do not follow the rules the ability to trade with other states in the global system. While the hegemonic power benefits by creating the rules, weaker states in the system also benefit by receiving both security and economic benefits from the hegemonic states. Thus, the states understand their roles within the global system, and the hegemon provides benefits to those states provided they operate within the rules established by the hegemon. Specifically, for scholars such as Gilpin (1981), the power of a hegemonic state creates both global stability and operative rules of interactions that reflect the preferences of the hegemonic state. More specifically, a hegemonic state will institutionalize a system of rules and institutions that preserve and advance its goals and values.

Both realist and hegemonic stability theorists understand the concept of international order in fundamentally different ways due to their assumptions of the nature of the global system. Realists understand global anarchy as a static concept that cannot be overcome, whereas hegemonic stability theorists believe that global anarchy is a given, but is not static. It can be overcome if there is a powerful enough state that can establish order. Therefore, scholars who have studied the concept of order have noted that there are basically two different ways to conceptualize global order in international relations. Realists, such as Waltz (1979, 89–92), state that international order is basically synonymous with the structure of the international system. Other realist scholars view international order as being synonymous with stability, which can only be achieved when there is a balance of power in the international system (Walt 1985). Specifically, Acharya (2007) argues that one way in which to conceptualize order is to examine the relative power capabilities of all of the states and assess the distribution of power. This is a descriptive and static conceptualization of order, which does not take into account the effect of order upon other states. It instead takes a snapshot of each state's power at a given time, giving a limited understanding of the global order based on the behavior of states.

There is a second way of conceptualizing international order that examines not only power distribution but also takes into account the rules established within the global order. Acharya (2007) states that international order is an increase in the level of stability and predictability within the international system. This conceptualization of global order is an outcome-oriented approach that is concerned more with stability and predictability than with the power distribution of states within the international system. Hegemonic stability theorists conceptualize international order in this way. They are concerned with the goal of establishing an order instead of just reflecting the international power structure.

Hegemonic stability theorists argue that a concentration of power in a specific state will inherently create order. In fact, the more powerful a state, the more likely it is to be able to create and maintain order. This is due to the fact that the hegemonic power has enough power to enforce its goals and rules. More specifically, hegemonic states actively strive to establish order to ensure that their goals are achieved and their rules are followed by the international system. When a hegemonic state is able to create an order, the order allows the hegemonic state to benefit through trade, and in exchange offers military protection and predictability in interactions to weaker states that are willing to accept the global order. Thus, Bull (2012, 8) argues that international order will sustain the primary goals of international society. In other words, if a hegemonic state is able to establish order, then it can create and sustain the primary goals of international society. Other scholars have noted that the institutionalization of a system of order is driven by the desire to

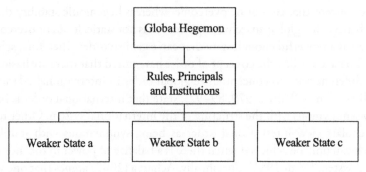

Fig. 1. International Order

organize the system to preserve the goals and values of the hegemonic state (Stewart-Ingersoll and Frazier 2012).

Ultimately, international order must be understood as a hegemonic state's rules and norms that are accepted by weaker states within the international system. Weaker states must abide by these rules and norms to receive benefits from the global hegemon. In other words, international order is a hierarchical relationship where the hegemon specifically establishes government through rules, principles, and institutions that govern the interactions between states (see fig. 1). More specifically, Stewart-Ingersoll and Frazier (2012, 18) argue that international order is made up of the "governing arrangements among the units of a system, including their rules, principles and institutions, which are designed to make interactions predictable and to sustain the goals and values that are collectively salient." Thus, an international order includes both a purpose and an organized means through which it is achieved, and the salient interests will be asymmetrically representative of the most influential actors in the system. This is especially so when the hegemonic power can effectively use coercive powers to ensure compliance with the international order.

As stated earlier, one of the benefits of creating an international order is that it makes interactions between states in that order more predictable (Stewart-Ingersoll and Frazier 2012). The hegemonic state establishes international order to benefit its own interests, namely trade and sustaining its own goals and values, whereas weaker states are interested in accepting the international order so that they have increased predictability in their interactions with the hegemonic state as well as with other states within the international order. Ideally, according to Bull (2002, 16–18), international order should contribute to four main rules, specifically, maintaining the status quo of the system of states (especially in regard to internal sovereignty), protecting the independence of states by recognizing territorial autonomy, trying to promote the absence of war between states, and ensuring that agreements between states in the global order are upheld. However, the specific rules that the hegemonic state institutes in creating international order depend on the goals and norms of the hegemonic power.

It should be noted that international order provided by a hegemon alleviates the problem of anarchy in international relations. Weaker states are not faced with the security dilemma, because as long as they play by the rules imposed by the hegemon, they can depend on predictability in interactions as well as the hegemon's protection of their independence and territorial autonomy.

International Order in a Bipolar System

The preceding discussion has focused on defining an international order where there is one global hegemon that is able to establish international order. A single state is able to become so powerful that it is able to establish the global order. This is often referred to as a unipolar system. For example, the United Kingdom was able to achieve global hegemonic status during the 19th century. Between 1815 and 1914, it established the order known as the Pax Britannica, where it set up a liberal trade empire. States had to abide by the rules set up by the British. In return, the British helped to suppress piracy and allow trade not only between the British and weaker powers but also between the weaker states in the global system. The United Kingdom was able to achieve unprecedented wealth by trading with other states, yet to ensure that trade routes were not disrupted by piracy, which would have diminished that wealth, the British had to ensure that their navy was strong enough to defeat any pirates that were a hindrance to global trade. The fact that the British navy fought pirates ensured that other states could also take advantage and gain wealth through trade. Thus, it was in the weaker states' interests to accept the British global order. In other words, as long as weaker states did not challenge the hegemonic power, the global order remained intact. Pax Britannica was able to last approximately a whole century.

Pax Britannica lasted until the rapid industrialization period of the early 20th century when Germany, Japan, and the United States became able to challenge the United Kingdom's status as the global hegemon. Germany, especially, wanted to challenge the United Kingdom as the global hegemon, and rapidly increased its spending during this period. While the United Kingdom was still the global hegemon, Germany was a revisionist state in that it wanted to revise the global power hierarchy and no longer wanted to be bound by the global order established by the United Kingdom. Germany's actions as a revisionist power led to its creation of alliances with other powers to try to balance against the power of the United Kingdom and to an effort to install itself as the global hegemon. Instead, World War I ensued, and a period of time more closely resembling a multipolar system came about. With the defeat of Germany in World War I, the United Kingdom tried to reestablish its dominance as the global hegemon, but was not able to fully achieve dominance again. Instead, Germany remained a revisionist state, and in part due to the harsh treatment that it received at the end of World War I, it was not long before Germany again challenged the global hierarchy through war. This led to World War II, which was devastating to the whole European continent. Most of the European states suffered great losses of life, economy, and power, and the United Kingdom could no longer even attempt to reinstate itself as the global hegemon.

Following World War II in 1945, two states emerged as being the most powerful in the global system. The United States and the Soviet Union had differing ideological views, and quickly set up an international order in each of their spheres of influence that reflected that ideology. They established rules and institutions that created order over their respective spheres of influence, with most of Western Europe falling under the order that the United States established, while Eastern Europe fell under the order established by the Soviet Union (see fig. 2). Figure 2 shows the makeup of the international order during the Cold War period. Both hegemonic powers attempted to expand their order over more of the system while limiting the other hegemon's ability to do so. In the United States, the government developed a policy of containment to try to prevent the spread of communism around the world. Both hegemonic states would attempt to weaken the other through proxy conflicts, attempting to decrease the other states' power. The United States fought in Korea, where China and the Soviet Union helped the North Koreans. Similarly, the United States fought in the Vietnam War against the North Vietnamese, who were aided by the Soviet Union. The Soviet Union, on the other hand, fought to fully establish communism in Afghanistan, and the United States aided the Muhajedin, who were fighting against the Soviets. Basically, both states tried to prevent each other from increasing the number of states that fell within each sphere of influence and thus the international order established within that sphere. Both sides attempted to prevent direct confrontation with each other, especially follow-

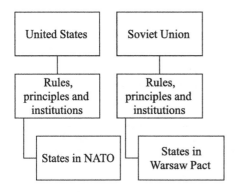

Fig. 2. Bipolar International Order

ing the Cuban Missile Crisis in 1962, understanding that a direct confrontation would lead to nuclear war and the distinct possibility of mutual destruction.

The preceding discussion has focused on the global system. Lemke (2002) argues that the global power hierarchy is often replicated at the regional level. More specifically, he states that regional great powers create a hierarchical regional structure that falls under the global hierarchical structure. In other words, while there is one global hegemon, regional powers that accept the rules established by the global hegemon are given the authority both to enforce the global rules and to establish a regional order by which the weaker states in a given region must abide. This regional hierarchical structure is very similar to the global hierarchical model. This is called the multiple hierarchy model. Therefore, we can adapt Lemke's (2002) model to determine how regional and international order are related (see fig. 3).

In the hypothetical example provided in figure 3, there is one global hegemon and two regional hegemons from different regions. Each of the two regional hegemons must create its own regional order, and the weaker regional states must follow the regional order established by the regional hegemons. In this hypothetical example, the regional hegemons must enact their regional order so that it does not conflict with the global order established by the global hegemon. There will thus be subtle differences in the regional orders established by regional powers in their respective regions. Further, we use the concept of regional hegemon according to Lemke (2002) and Slobodchikoff (2014) to denote the strongest regional power. This is not the way that Mearsheimer (2001) conceptualizes the term "regional hegemon." Whereas Mearsheimer (2001) argues that a regional hegemon can have global reach and is the most powerful in different regions, Lemke (2002) and Slobodchikoff (2014) distinguish between a global hegemon

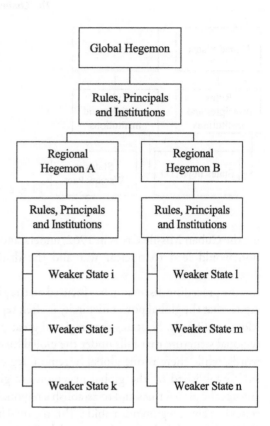

Fig. 3. Global and Regional Hierarchical Order

and a regional hegemon. According to Lemke (2002) and Slobodchikoff (2014), a regional hegemon is the strongest power in a specific region, whereas the global hegemon is the strongest power globally. When the United States has more power than India, for example, the United States would be the global hegemon and India would be the regional hegemon in South Asia. Thus, in a unipolar system, there is a single global hegemon, and each region has its own regional hegemon. In a bipolar system, there are two hegemons that control their blocs, and there are regional hegemons supporting the hegemon in control of their bloc. In a multipolar system, there is no global hegemon, merely regional hegemons vying for control.

During the Cold War, the bipolar global and regional hierarchies would look similar to figure 3, except there would be two global hegemons. The regional hegemons in each sphere of influence would establish regional order that would comply with the global order established by its global hegemon.

The Problem of Reach

In a unipolar system, it is assumed that the global hegemon is able to project enough power to cover the entire system. However, this doesn't take into account geography and the fact that there are some places where a hegemon cannot realistically project its power. For example, it would be incorrect to assume that the United States can project just as much power in Sri Lanka as it does in Mexico. Therefore, some scholars have argued that power projection can be measured geographically, and that it is possible to determine where a hegemon is not able to project its power (Boulding 1962; Bueno de Mesquita 1981; Lemke 2002). Further, there are certain geographical zones that are referred to as power vacuums, where hierarchical relationships between states do not dominate (Rhamey, Slobodchikoff, and Volgy 2015). In these geographical zones, there is no global order imposed by the global hegemon, but rather there is jockeying among regional powers to establish a regional order that may or may not be nested within the global order.

In geographical spaces where there is a global power vacuum, regional powers will try to establish their own rules, principles, and institutions. These may or may not mirror the order established by the global hegemon, since the hegemon would not be able to enforce the global rules. Further, since the global hegemon would not have the reach to be able to establish rules and predictability, it is more likely that low-level conflict between regional states would occur. Regional powers would be more likely to enter into conflict over the right to develop the regional rules, principles, and institutions and thus establish regional order.

Once regional order is established within a hierarchical global power vacuum, then the hierarchical structure of order will resemble figure 3, minus the global order. There would just be a regional hierarchical structure of order, with weaker states within the region following the order established by the regional hegemon instead of the global order established by the global hegemon.

The whole preceding discussion has focused on the creation of global order according to hegemonic stability theory in both a unipolar and a bipolar system. Ultimately, the key to hegemonic stability theory is that the systemic power structure cannot change. In other words, the systemic rules remain in effect providing that the hegemon can enforce them. If there is a change in the systemic power structure, where the hegemon loses the ability to enforce the rules that it has established, then the system becomes more anarchic and thus unstable. It is important to note that hegemonic stability is in direct conflict with neorealism in that hegemonic stability theory argues that the global system is most stable under a unipolar system, whereas neorealism argues that the global system is most stable under a bipolar system. However, it is natural to question what happens as the global hegemon begins to lose its share of power in the systemic power structure.

Global Order and Power Transition Theory

The answer to the question of what happens as a hegemonic state loses relative power in the systemic power structure is addressed by power transition theory. Specifically, power transition theorists argue that conflict is more likely as the global hegemon loses power relative to other states in the system (Organski 1958; Organski and Kugler 1981; DiCicco and Levy 1999). It is important to note that power transition theory identifies the hegemon and a revisionist state. The revisionist state must be dissatisfied with the status quo and the rules established by the global hegemon. In contrast, a status quo state is a state that accepts the global order and is happy with the order and rules established by the hegemonic state. It does not seek to overturn or challenge the global order. The revisionist state, however, does not want to accept the order established by the global hegemon. The revisionist state will work to overturn the international order in two ways. First, the revisionist state must increase its own power vis-à-vis the global hegemon, and, second, the revisionist state will ally itself with other revisionist states to attempt to balance the power of the hegemonic power and bring about change in the international order. In other words, not only must a revisionist state be dissatisfied with the status quo and the systemic rules of behavior, it must increase its power relative to the global hegemon while also allying with other revisionist powers.

Similar to hegemonic stability theory, power transition theory argues that the most stable global system is unipolar. For example, power transition theorists would argue that the United States was the undisputed global hegemon immediately after World War II, and that the Soviet Union was a dissatisfied state that wished to challenge the United States' hegemonic status (Wohlforth 1994). In fact, some scholars have noted that the Soviet Union was never in fact a bipolar power (Wohlforth 1994), and others have found that the most stable and peaceful periods during the Cold War were where there was a higher level of hegemonic power than during periods of relative power parity (Volgy and Imwalle 1995).

According to Lemke (2002), power transition theory applies at the regional level as well. The regional hegemon establishes the regional order nested within the global order, and the weaker states choose to be either status quo states, accepting the regional order, or revisionist states that would work to overturn the regional order. At the global level, it is important to examine the great powers and regional hegemons to determine which states are status quo states and which states are revisionist states. At the regional level, it is important to examine the weaker states to determine if they are status quo or revisionist states. The reason it is important to know this is because while the global and regional hegemons establish their respective orders, the order is only stable as long as the powerful states within the order accept the order as being legitimate. In other words, if a global hegemon establishes an international order and the regional hegemons do not accept the legitimacy of the international order, then the regional hegemons will ally themselves with other powerful revisionist powers in an effort to change the international order. Similarly, the powers in a regional order must accept the regional order established by the regional hegemon for that order to be stable. Some powerful states may look to the hegemonic power to entice them to accept the international order. These states are not fully status quo, but neither are they fully revisionist. They lean toward the status quo (see table 1). Similarly, a state can lean toward being a revisionist state, but it needs more enticement by the revisionist states to be fully revisionist. Finally, a state can choose not to ally itself with any other powers, or to ally itself with all of the major powers (both status quo and revisionist) in the international order. This is an undecided state. Table 1 categorizes the choices that regional powers must make in accepting or attempting to reject the international order.

The second half of the 20th century and the first two decades of the 21st century saw a prolonged period of great change in the international order. The international order evolved from a multipolar system at the end of World War I, to a bipolar system arising from the ashes of World War II, to a unipolar system following the end of the Cold War. We now turn to a discussion of the evolution of the global order following the end of World War II to the emergence and subsequent decline of the power of the global hegemon in the international order.

Evolution of the Global Order after World War II

World War II left most of the European powers as shells of the powers that they had been at the turn of the 20th century. Only two powers emerged

Table 1. Categorization of Status Quo vs. Revisionist Power

Solid Status Quo	Leans Status Quo	Undecided	Leans Revisionist	Solid Revisionist
Institutionalized Cooperative Relationship with US	Institutionalized Cooperative Relationship with US	Either no institutionalized cooperative relationships **OR** Institutionalized Cooperative Relationship with both the United States (major status quo power) and Russia (major revisionist power)	Institutionalized Cooperative Relationship with Russia	Institutionalized Cooperative Relationship with Russia
Institutionalized Cooperative Relationship with UK	Ad hoc or Institutionalized Relationship with EU		Ad hoc or Institutionalized Relationship with China	Institutionalized Cooperative Relationship with China
Institutionalized Cooperative Relationship with France	Ad hoc or Institutionalized Relationship with France _or_ Germany		Lacks Institutionalized Cooperative Relationship with US	
Institutionalized Cooperative Relationship with Germany	Ad hoc or Institutionalized Relationship with Japan			
Institutionalized Cooperative Relationship with EU				
Institutionalized Cooperative Relationship with Japan				
Lacks Institutionalized Cooperative Relationship with Russia				

that were strong enough global powers to establish international order. Specifically, the United States and the Soviet Union both had enough power to establish an international order, yet neither power was strong enough to defeat the other. While both powers had allied themselves with the other Allied powers during World War II, both Washington and Moscow realized that by the end of the war they would be the only two global powers left standing.

At the Yalta Conference in February 1945, US president Franklin D. Roosevelt, the prime minister of the United Kingdom, Winston Churchill, and Soviet premier Josef Stalin discussed the post–World War II world. Each leader had his own agenda that he wanted to see enacted. Roosevelt wanted Soviet agreement to join the United States in the war against Japan. Churchill wanted an agreement that would ensure free and fair democratic elections across all of Europe. Stalin wanted to establish spheres of influence for the great powers, which would allow the creation of buffer states; this would protect the Soviet Union from another attack from Germany the way Russia had been invaded by Germany in World War I and the Soviet Union had been invaded in World War II.

In addition, all of the leaders wanted to ensure that Germany would no longer be a threat in the future. Thus, they began to discuss the partitioning of Germany into occupation zones. Each major power would receive a part of Germany to control. Since French general Charles de Gaulle had not been invited, Stalin insisted that a French partition of Germany would have to come out of the United States' and United Kingdom's sections.

To gain concessions from both Churchill and Roosevelt, Stalin agreed to allow Eastern European states to create democratic institutions according to democratic principles. It was extremely important to Churchill that all of Central and Eastern Europe, especially Poland, establish democratic institutions. Even though Stalin agreed to this, he reiterated to both leaders how important it was to the security of the Soviet Union that Poland not be able to serve as a corridor for attack from a Western power. Poland had been twice used as a corridor to attack the Soviet Union (once during World War I, when it was the Russian Empire, and the second time when Adolf Hitler invaded the Soviet Union during World War II).

To alleviate Stalin's concerns, Churchill and Roosevelt agreed to use the basic structure of the communist provisional government that had been installed by Stalin, but they argued that the provisional government had to be reorganized according to democratic principles. Stalin agreed to this point. Further, he agreed to Roosevelt's request that the Soviet Union join the war against Japan a couple of months after the end of the war against

Germany in exchange for postwar concessions from the United States, which Roosevelt accepted. Despite being attacked domestically for the Yalta agreement, both Churchill and Roosevelt insisted that Stalin could be trusted to fulfill his side of the agreement.

Following the conference at Yalta, it quickly became clear that Stalin would not fulfill his end of the agreement in Poland. In fact, the United States ambassador to the Soviet Union cabled Washington and stated that he was concerned that Stalin's plans for Poland were nothing short of totalitarianism, and not in the least bit democratic. Roosevelt had to agree that he had been mistaken in his trust of Stalin, and that he could no longer believe that Stalin was an ally of the United States.

Relations between the former allies continued to sour after the war, with the Soviet Union continuing to install communist governments in Eastern Europe while consolidating its power. The Soviets were driven by the desire to create their sphere of influence and a buffer zone, thus protecting them from possible attack from powerful Western European countries. One of the important aspects of Soviet control was dismantling any democratic elements and ensuring that the states in the region would owe their allegiance to the Soviet hegemonic state. In other words, the Soviet Union was in the process of establishing a regional order, with it being the regional hegemon, and the weaker states having to accept the rules and the order.

During this period, the United States and the United Kingdom were also working to create their own vision of a world order, that of a liberal international order. While the Soviets had reluctantly agreed to join the United Nations providing that they had a way to veto significant decisions through the United Nations Security Council, the rest of the liberal international order was designed to favor the United States and its ideology. The United Kingdom, which had been the global hegemon, began to cede more and more of its status to the United States, relinquishing its right to establish the regional order to Washington.

At the heart of the new liberal order established by the United States was the rights of the individual and the spread of democracy. All of the institutions established by the Bretton Woods system were designed to help the liberal ideology spread through monetary institutions such as the World Bank and the International Monetary Fund. The basic belief during the immediate aftermath of World War II was that not only was it imperative that another world war not break out, but that the United States had to assert its power globally as opposed to what it had done after World War I by withdrawing from the global order and its position of prominence as a hegemon. After World War II, the United States embraced its position as the regional hegemon in the Western Hemisphere. Similar to the Soviet Union, Washington realized that it needed to maintain a sphere of influence and to ensure that it maintained its hegemonic power within that sphere of influence.

By 1946, it became apparent that there was a definite break between the former allies. Two regional hegemons had emerged with competing visions of a global order. In a famous speech in Fulton, Missouri, Winston Churchill emphatically stated, "The United States stands at this time at the pinnacle of world power. It is a solemn moment for the American democracy" (Churchill 2009). This statement established the regional hegemony of the United States. His most famous statement from the speech was the following:

> From Stettin in the Baltic to Trieste in the Adriatic an iron curtain has descended across the Continent. Behind that line lie all the capitals of the ancient states of Central and Eastern Europe. Warsaw, Berlin, Prague, Vienna, Budapest, Belgrade, Bucharest and Sofia; all these famous cities and the populations around them lie in what I must call the Soviet sphere, and all are subject, in one form or another, not only to Soviet influence but to a very high and in some cases increasing measure of control from Moscow. (Churchill 2009)

This speech was a rallying cry to the American public, urging them to stay in the position of power as the regional hegemon, and urging Washington and the American public that it had to remain in Europe as the only alternative to the communist ideology propagated by Moscow. Further, Churchill made it clear that he thought that Moscow was not interested in a war against the United States and its British allies, but that it only respected military strength from its ideological adversary, and thus Washington had to prepare for a long ideological struggle against a determined foe. The speech heralded a new chapter in the post–World War II era, that of a bipolar system.

Churchill's speech was just a reiteration of a policy that Washington was developing, understanding that it had to ensure its newly acquired hegemonic status. In February 1946, George Kennan, an official in the United States Embassy in Moscow, answered a query from the United States Department of State, in which the embassy staff was asked how to develop policy toward the Soviet Union following World War II. In what became known as the "Long Telegram," George Kennan wrote that the seeds of the destruction of the Soviet Union lay within communism itself. He stated that the only way communism could be dangerous is that it could spread to other countries and thus remain a viable ideology. If it was isolated and not allowed to spread, he believed that it would self-destruct (Kennan [1946] 1991).

Kennan's "Long Telegram" helped create a policy toward the Soviet Union that became known as "containment." His telegram to Washington had instilled a fear in policy makers that if communism spread to one country, that it would then spread to another country. This became known as domino theory, in which one state falling to communism would lead to another falling, to another falling, until communism had spread so far that it would become impossible to defeat the ideology. While Kennan's telegram urged that the United States use trade and money to bolster capitalist markets to ensure that they would not fall to communism, policy makers believed they needed to use both economic and military means to prevent the spread of communism.

Ultimately, both Churchill's "Iron Curtain" speech and Kennan's "Long Telegram" heralded a new type of war, one that was not fought directly, but one in which there was severe competition, an arms race, dueling collective security organizations, and proxy wars to prevent the ideological opponent from gaining an upper hand in a struggle for hegemonic domination. In short, these two events illustrated the beginning of the Cold War between two regional hegemons, the United States and the Soviet Union.

The Cold War was remarkable for the fact that the two great powers never fought directly against each other. Instead, there was fierce competition to ensure that other states in the system would accept the order established by each of the regional great powers. In Europe, the United States established the Marshall Plan to reconstruct Germany following World War II. This ensured that the United States would be active in Europe. Further, the establishment of NATO (the North Atlantic Treaty Organization) as a collective security organization achieved three major objectives for both the United States and Western Europe. First, it kept the United States active and engaged in Western Europe. Second, it kept the Soviet Union out of Western Europe, ensuring that it could maintain its regional order. Finally, it ensured that Germany would not be able to increase its power again to the point that it would be dangerous enough to begin a new world war.

In the rest of the world, the United States and the Soviet Union competed to convince other states to accept their respective regional orders. Weaker states were often forced to choose to align themselves with one power or the other. This competition between the regional powers was often intense, leading to proxy wars, where each side would aid regional actors in conflicts against the other regional hegemon. For example, in Vietnam, the Soviet Union aided the North Vietnamese against the South Vietnamese allied with the United States. While the Soviet Union did not actively deploy many military forces, they did send special forces as consultants and supplied the North Vietnamese with weapons to use against the United States military. Similarly, when the Soviet Union invaded Afghanistan, the United

States sent military advisers and weapons to aid the Mujahidin in their conflict against the Soviet army.

Interestingly, the weaker states also used the bipolar system to their advantage. Weaker states discovered that they could play the great powers off each other to achieve their own goals (Cooley 2012). As long as they didn't overstep their negotiating ability, they could create a bidding war between the two powers to determine their global alignment. However, once they had aligned themselves, they couldn't easily switch loyalties.

Ultimately, on each continent, the great powers competed against each other in an effort to defeat their adversary. These states were vital to maintaining the global power of each hegemon. Therefore, in a sense, the states could request benefits from the rival hegemons, knowing that they were in a sense playing kingmaker. However, they knew that there would still be two rival powers and that the bipolar system was unlikely to change. Further, regional states that maintained a rivalry with another regional state often chose to align themselves with opposing rival hegemons in an effort to gain power in their own strategic rivalry. For example, in South Asia, India maintained better relations with the Soviet Union, choosing to buy their weapons and cooperate more closely with the Soviets than with the United States. Pakistan, India's regional rival, chose to align itself more closely with the United States than with the Soviet Union. Both India and Pakistan looked for an advantage in their alignment that would help them gain an advantage over the other rival.

On March 11, 1985, history was made in the Soviet Union. The Communist Party of the Soviet Union elected Mikhail Sergeevich Gorbachev as the general secretary of the Central Committee of the Communist Party of the Soviet Union. His election set in motion a tumultuous set of events that would profoundly impact the whole world. While Yuri Andropov had advocated for Gorbachev to succeed him as the general secretary, the Central Committee was very wary of giving the reins of power to someone who was born after the Russian Revolution and the Russian Civil War. They believed that he did not have the same ties to the revolutionary philosophy that his predecessors possessed. Therefore, when Andropov died, the Central Committee elected Konstantin Chernenko as general secretary. Chernenko was part of the old elite, and had lived through the Revolution and Civil War. Chernenko was very old and terminally ill, however. His election was considered a compromise between those who wanted Gorbachev and those who were reluctant to let someone who had not lived through the Revolution and Civil War lead the country.

The election of Chernenko over Gorbachev to replace Andropov illustrated the generational gap between the party elite and the younger successors. It had long been noted that the party elite was getting older, yet was reluctant to relinquish power, and thus a power struggle between the generations was inevitable (Bialer 1982). Chernenko was seen as a chance for the older party elite to determine whether or not Gorbachev would be suitable to lead in a new era. However, Chernenko was only in power for 13 months before he died. Thus, on March 11, 1985, the Communist Party of the Soviet Union decided to elect Gorbachev as the new general secretary of the Central Committee of the Communist Party of the Soviet Union, realizing that it was time to usher in a new era for the Soviet Union while hoping that he wouldn't upset the balance of power too greatly.

Gorbachev's ascension to the position of general secretary of the Central Committee of the Communist Party of the Soviet Union was a critical turning point in the history of the Soviet Union. Unlike his predecessors, Gorbachev recognized the fact that the Soviet Union had stagnated and was not evolving toward the ideal communist state envisioned by Vladimir Lenin. The economy had stagnated under Leonid Brezhnev, and continued its stagnation under Andropov and Chernenko. Gorbachev recognized that the Soviet Union would destroy itself unless the economy was revitalized.

According to Gorbachev, one of the main problems with the economy was the fact that the people no longer worked hard to build their country. They had grown complacent, and no longer had the drive to ensure the survival of Soviet ideals. He recognized that the planned economy of the Soviet Union had to be reformed to increase productivity instead of maintaining stagnation. He argued that there was little incentive for the workers to produce more than they were supposed to according to quotas established by the government. If they produced more than the quota, they were punished by receiving a higher quota for the next time period. If they did not produce their quota, they were punished by the government. Therefore, the incentive for the workers was to produce just enough to fulfill the quota without taking any initiative to try to increase productivity. Further, he argued that the incentive structure of the Soviet Union not only stifled productivity but also encouraged workers to turn to alcoholism as they no longer strived to improve the Soviet Union. In turn, the increase in alcoholism in the Soviet Union only aggravated the country's productivity problem.

In short, Gorbachev realized that a massive rebuilding of the Soviet economy was the only way to save the Soviet Union from certain demise. In fact, Gorbachev saw this as the only way to reach the ideals of the Russian Revolution (Gorbachev 1987a, 1987b). Thus, in 1986, Gorbachev instituted a new set of reforms that he called "perestroika," literally translated as restructuring.

However, Gorbachev realized that he would face significant opposition to his perestroika reforms from the political elites, and thus instituted reforms that would make perestroika more accessible and transparent to the masses, which would in turn make the reforms so popular that the political elite would not be able to oppose the reforms (Gibbs 1999; McNair 2006). Specifically, the transparency associated with perestroika was referred to as "glasnost," which comes from the old Russian word for voice. Thus, glasnost gave voice to reforms underway in the Soviet Union.

The Cold War continued until approximately 1988, when both the United States and the Soviet Union both decided to negotiate to end the conflict (Matlock 2004). Both US president Ronald Reagan and Soviet president Mikhail Gorbachev had developed enough of a relationship that they had built up enough trust to begin the process of negotiating the end of the Cold War. The most important shift that occurred was a shift in ideological thinking that the two rival ideologies were inevitably on a collision course. Reagan no longer saw communism as a threat, and Gorbachev came to believe in self-determination.

In November 1989, groups of Germans gathered at the Berlin Wall, demanding to be allowed through the checkpoints to visit West Berlin. The border guards were confused as they did not have specific orders about how to handle the groups of people. They began to let people through the checkpoints. As word got out, more and more people gathered at the wall. People began to climb the wall and call to others on the other side of the wall. A wall that had once served as a symbol of the "Iron Curtain" and the separation between the two international orders established by the United States and the Soviet Union was taken down. Very quickly after the collapse of the wall, Germany was reunited.

Due to Germany's past history in World War I and World War II, both the United States and the Soviet Union were concerned about the unification of Germany. Discussions between the three parties centered upon what would happen to the soldiers stationed in Germany. Neither the Soviet Union nor the United States wanted there to be no presence of foreign troops in Germany to ensure that Germany would not remilitarize. Instead, Gorbachev agreed to withdraw Soviet forces from East Germany and allow a unified Germany to join NATO providing that NATO not expand further east than the borders of Germany. President George H. W. Bush, Secretary of State James Baker, and German chancellor Helmut Kohl all verbally assured Gorbachev that NATO would not expand beyond Germany's borders (Sarotte 2010).

After the fall of the Berlin Wall, states that had been in the Soviet sphere of influence in Central and Eastern Europe began to assert their independence from Soviet control. Very quickly, the Soviet Union lost control of these satellite states and began to retreat to its own borders. Just two short years after the fall of the Berlin Wall, the Soviet Union collapsed. Gorbachev was deposed as president of the Soviet Union, and in its stead were 15 newly independent states. Only one hegemon was left standing. Almost overnight, the global system went from bipolar to unipolar.

In the United States, euphoria over the collapse of the Soviet Union led many policy makers to assume that the United States had won the Cold War and had not negotiated its cessation. Further, the collapse of the Soviet Union led to a scenario where no country could effectively stand up to US hegemony. Whereas previously Washington had to court weaker states to convince them to join the liberal order, following the collapse of the Soviet Union, Washington no longer had to court or listen to its allies. It was the only hegemonic power with no competition. It no longer had to have the support of the regional powers. Instead, Washington believed that, since it was the global hegemon with the only surviving order, all of the other states would remain content with the world order. It believed that even those states that had been a part of the Soviet regional order would be content to join and support the liberal order. Indeed, through the last decade of the 20th century, Washington's calculations were correct. The vast majority of the states in the global system adapted to the liberal order including Russia (the successor state to the Soviet Union).

Fearing a resurgent Russia, many of the Central and Eastern European states were extremely enthusiastic about joining the liberal order. They quickly moved to convert command economies into market economies, and began to request NATO membership. Despite the fact that NATO's main purpose had been to protect Europe from the threat of the Soviet Union and that the Soviet Union no longer existed, the United States seriously began to consider expanding the Atlantic alliance. Any verbal promises about not expanding NATO further east than Germany's borders were long forgotten, as the United States, as the global hegemon, believed that it had the right and the duty to spread democracy and security to states that were formerly a part of the Soviet Union's regional order.

Over the vocal opposition of the Russians, NATO proceeded to expand to the east. The Russians did not have the power to stop it. Russia had proposed to the United States a conference on European security that could create a new organization responsible for collective security in Europe that would involve both the Russians and the Americans, but Washington rejected such an offer. Moscow believed that Washington was relegating it to a minor regional power status unlike the power that it had wielded at the height of the Cold War when Washington was concerned with Moscow's actions. Moscow began to sour on the global order, but it did not have enough power to become a revisionist state.

During this period, China was continuing to grow into an economic juggernaut. Although it was concerned with the political and democratic aspects of the liberal order, Beijing accepted many economic aspects of the liberal order, recognizing that it needed to take an active role in the global economy even if it actively avoided many of the political and democratizing aspects of the liberal order (Slobodchikoff 2017a).

On September 11, 2001, the United States came under attack. Terrorists hijacked planes and used them as missiles against the World Trade Center in New York City (a symbol of the United States' economic hegemony) and the Pentagon in Washington, DC (a symbol of the United States' military hegemony). While Washington had begun a very slight retrenchment during the first part of George W. Bush's presidency in 2001, the attacks of September 11 illustrated to policy makers that the United States had no choice but to become even more engaged in the world and take the war against terror to the terrorists instead of waiting for the terrorists to directly attack the United States. During this period, the Bush Doctrine was formed in which President Bush stated that it was time for states to directly choose. Either they would support the United States and accept the liberal order or they would be considered to be against the United States and the liberal order, and thus be considered enemies. In fact, in January, 2002, Bush directly named three countries as the Axis of Evil, or states that actively were against the United States and the liberal order. These states were North Korea, Iran, and Iraq.

While Washington needed allies to help in the war on terror in Afghanistan, it needed these allies for specific purposes. For example, Washington needed Moscow's help to negotiate the use of airbases in Central Asia from which to conduct operations and maintain supply routes. Washington needed Pakistan and its intelligence services to help determine the location of the terrorists in Afghanistan. However, Washington was very goal oriented. It needed results, and was less willing to provide for the needs of allied states within the liberal order. Ideology was no longer important. Instead, expediency and necessity began to control Washington's foreign policy. It no longer took into account the views of other states, instead moving with a determination that, since it was the hegemonic power, its decisions would be final.

Following the terrorist attacks in 2001, Russian president Vladimir Putin offered to cooperate with Washington on counterterrorism and sharing intelligence that would lead to defeating Al Qaeda and other terrorist groups. Moscow had its own issues with Islamic terrorism, especially from the breakaway region of Chechnya. Moscow also agreed to allow overflights of its territory by American aircraft in the war against the Taliban in Afghanistan. This was unprecedented, as just a few years earlier, Moscow would have ordered any US military plane shot down if it had entered Soviet airspace.

Cooperation between the two former adversaries was relatively short lived. President George W. Bush announced that the United States would withdraw from the Anti-Ballistic Missile (ABM) Treaty. The ABM Treaty had been one of the most important cooperative treaties between the Soviet Union and the United States. Signed in 1972, the ABM Treaty prohibited either state from constructing missile defenses against long-range nuclear weapons. The idea was that if both powers retained the ability to destroy the other side with nuclear weapons, then neither side would be willing to do so because it would be mutually assured destruction. Withdrawing from the ABM Treaty was taken as further evidence that Washington no longer believed that Russia was a great power that was worthy of respect in the global order. Instead, this action signaled that Washington believed Russia to be a weak regional power that had no place in the global hierarchy of power. The United States allowed the ABM Treaty to expire in June 2002 without it being renegotiated.

During the period following the September 11 attacks, Washington lost sight of geopolitics, and the importance of state actors, instead focusing on its conflict with nonstate actors. Washington's power as a global hegemon was in decline, and it no longer focused as much attention on maintaining the liberal order. For example, the US decided that it could use the September 11 attacks as an excuse to invade and defeat Iraq, an old adversary. Iraq had long been a problem for the United States, and there were those in Washington who argued that it had to be dealt with before it became a direct threat.

The events of September 11, 2001 had conditioned Washington to be more aggressive in its foreign policy by trying to prevent a possible crisis through force rather than having to react to a crisis after having been attacked. Bush argued that it was better to invade and take control of the weapons of mass destruction that Saddam Hussein was thought to possess than be taken by surprise by an attack from those weapons within the US. Thus, despite international pressure not to invade, the United States and several allies, including the United Kingdom and countries in Eastern Europe, chose to invade Iraq.

The following year, in 2004, NATO again expanded, this time to include the Baltic states, which had once been part of the Soviet Union. Moscow again raised a significant protest, but again was unable to muster enough power to prevent NATO from expanding. Despite Moscow's protests, NATO began holding talks with Georgia in 2005 on the likelihood of Georgia joining the alliance, and in February 2005, both states signed a Partnership for Peace Agreement, which began the process of bringing Georgia into the alliance. Further, in 2008, the Bucharest Summit promised Georgia eventual membership in NATO. Also, in 2008, Ukraine officially requested a NATO Membership Action Plan, which is the first formal step to joining NATO.

It should be noted that not all of the NATO member states were in agreement about pursuing rapid expansion of NATO. While the United States and Poland were actively pushing to expand NATO, both France and Germany were worried about Russian opposition and were worried that Russia would treat expansion as a threat to its own security, and that this would cause serious problems in their relations with Russia in the future.

Ultimately, US foreign policy during this period was very US centric, with little regard for the desires or concerns of traditional allies. Washington was not concerned about the fact that other states in the international order were becoming more and more disillusioned with the liberal international order, and states such as Russia became revisionist states, with an active agenda of trying to create an alternative to the liberal order.

Russia was not the only state that became dissatisfied with the global order. China also had been increasingly showing signs of becoming dissatisfied with the global order and unipolarity. China had been challenging the United States in the South China Sea, and had been expanding its influence in Central and South America as well as in Africa. Officially, both China and Russia had stated that they favored a multipolar system as opposed to the unipolar system with the United States at its helm. In fact, on May 15, 1997, the Russian and the Chinese permanent UN diplomatic missions presented an official declaration for the United Nations Security Council and General Assembly of an intent to create a multipolar world and thus create a new international security structure.[1]

Despite using rhetoric claiming that they were in favor of a multipolar system, neither Russia nor China could directly take on US power. They each had to begin to challenge US power at the periphery, such as Moscow orchestrating efforts for Kyrgyzstan to force American troops to leave the Manas Airbase in that country or Beijing creating new islands in the South China Sea. However, even working together, Moscow and Beijing would not be strong enough to directly challenge US power. They had to work within the confines of existing organizations such as the Shanghai Cooperation Organi-

---

1. https://digitallibrary.un.org/record/234074?ln=en

zation as well as an effort to convince other countries to join them in an effort to balance against US power to create a multipolar system.

One of the main countries that both Beijing and Moscow had to target was India. India was the classic status quo power. Despite having allied itself with Moscow during the Cold War, India had received prominence during both George W. Bush's and Barack Obama's presidencies as Washington sought to keep its hegemonic status. The United States realized that it had to overcome decades of adversarial US foreign policies. Both Bush and Obama realized that they needed India and its growing economy as an important ally to prevent China and Russia from developing too much power and more importantly the ability to challenge the unipolar system.

Russia and China also recognized the importance of India and gaining India as a valuable ally in countering American hegemony. If there was to be a viable challenge to US hegemony, Moscow and Beijing had to convince India that it needed to ally itself with them. Beginning in 2002, the leaders of the three states have held yearly summits to increase cooperation between the three states. In fact, the tripartite meetings in 2017 reiterated that all three states were interested in creating a global system based on international law and moving toward a multipolar system.[2]

While India very much prefers the status quo, it also has a lifelong penchant for multilateralism (that first began under the leadership of Nehru as independent India's first prime minister). Similar to China, with the exception of grave human rights violations, India prefers noninterventionism in the domestic affairs of other states. If and when intervention is carried out, India has supported a multilateral coalition versus unilateral actions by superpowers. The United States has preferred a unilateral course of action in international affairs for the past few decades; it has exercised force without the consent of the United Nations. The United States has also bullied smaller powers economically as well as politically.

While Russia and China are indeed dissatisfied states in the current global order, India is still in play for both the United States on one side and Russia and China on the other. Indeed, it has become the lynchpin in determining the future of the global system. However, it is not obvious which powers are supported by India. India's support is vital for the United States if it wants to maintain the liberal order. As General Michael Hayden, former

---

2. C. Uday Bhaskar, "Russia-India-China Meeting Shows a Multipolar World Order Is Taking Shape," *South China Morning Post*, December 15, 2017, http://www.scmp.com/comment/insight-opinion/article/2124329/russia-india-china-meeting-shows-multipolar-world-order

director of both the US Central Intelligence Agency and the National Security Agency, stated, "There is now a battle for the formation of the next global order. Russia and China are battling to create a new global order, while the United States is fighting to continue its primacy in the liberal order." In fact, in the National Security Strategy of the United States of America (2017), the United States recognizes the importance of India in the global order, stating, "We welcome India's emergence as a leading global power and stronger strategic and defense partner. We will seek to increase quadrilateral cooperation with Japan, Australia, and India" (White House 2017). However, despite India's centrality to determining the viability of the global order, it is unclear as to where India stands in relation to the global order. India has publicly acknowledged the importance of its relationships with both the United States and Russia. It is a member of BRICS (Brazil, Russia, India, China, and South Africa), and a founding member of the New Development Bank. In fact, India was the first state to propose the New Development Bank as an alternative to the International Monetary Fund and the World Bank Group.

India is also a member of the Shanghai Cooperation Organization, which is a regional cooperation organization that focuses on security and terrorism, but has expanded to the economy and trade. The Shanghai Cooperation Organization has also been accused of undermining US interests in Central Asia and not spreading democratic values and not valuing human rights (Commission on Security and Operation in Europe 2006).

In this book, we examine India's place in the global order. Specifically, we examine whether it is a status quo power and content with the current world order, or a revisionist power that is interested in allying itself with other revisionist powers to balance against the United States and the liberal world order. It is possible to ascertain India's preference by examining its bilateral relationships with those great powers that are status quo states as well as those powers that are revisionist states. Using treaties and treaty networks, we find that India leans revisionist, but is not fully so. It still seems to be in the process of determining its position in the world order, and is allowing other states to court support from India.

In chapter 2, we examine the methodology that we use to determine India's standing in the global order. We specifically explain why we examine bilateral treaties, and introduce the concepts of treaty nesting and treaty networks. Understanding the relationships between the bilateral treaties is essential to determine the level of cooperation between India and other states, thus providing a way of determining the level of India's support for the global order.

3 • Treaty Networks and Determining State Preferences for the Global Order

In the previous chapter, we discussed the importance of the global order and India's place as a major power within that global order.[1] As a major power, India has a central role to play in helping to determine whether the current liberal global order is maintained in its current form or if the current challenge to the global order presented by China and Russia will be successful. To determine this, we have to determine India's preference for the status quo or revisionism. Is it a status quo power that aligns itself with the United States and its liberal allies in protecting the liberal global order, or is it a revisionist power that will help to hasten a change in the global order? Table 2 categorizes current major powers as either status quo or revisionist along with their positions in the global hierarchy. The powers that support the status quo tend to support the United States through UN votes, join multilateral organizations supported by the United States such as NATO, and support the United States by sending military and aid and sometimes troops to its armed conflicts such as in the war in Iraq or Afghanistan. In fact, most of the status quo powers have been supporters and allied with the United States since the end of World War II, when the United States became a hegemonic power. These states were allied with the United States in the bipolar system during the Cold War, and they continued to remain allied with United States in the post–Cold War order when the United States became the unilateral global hegemon.

In contrast to the status quo powers are the revisionist powers. These are

---

1. There has been much debate over whether India is a regional power, an emerging power, or a great power. For more on this debate, see Nayar and Paul (2003) and Pardesi (2015). For the purpose of our study, we argue that whether India is an important regional power, an emerging power, or a current great power, India is instrumental in helping to decide the future of the global order. Thus, for this study, we maintain that India is an important power.

Table 2. Status Quo vs. Revisionist Powers

Status Quo Powers	Revisionist Powers
United States of America (Global Hegemon)	China (Challenging for Hegemonic Status)
United Kingdom (Major Power)	Russia (Major Power)
France and Germany	Iran (Major Regional Power)
(Major European Powers)	
Japan (Major Regional Power)	

powers that are actively seeking to revise the global order and create a multi-polar systemic order as opposed to a unipolar order (Basrur 2011). As table 2 shows, the main revisionist powers are China, Russia, and Iran. China is actively attempting to challenge the United States' hegemonic status through its Belt and Road Initiative. Russia, with a rival to the United States, is also seeking to revise the global order. While Russia does not have the power to challenge the power of the United States, it can assist China in Beijing's efforts to challenge the global order. Finally, while Russia and China are major global powers, Iran is a regional power with the ability to challenge the status quo powers within its region.

The question naturally arises as to India's position within this framework. Is India a status quo power, or is it a revisionist power? We argue that India's foreign policy preferences and thus its position within the global order are determined by its levels of cooperation with either status quo or revisionist states. If India has higher levels of institutionalized cooperation with status quo states than with revisionist states, then it is a status quo power. If India maintains a higher level of institutionalized cooperation with revisionist powers than with status quo powers, then India is a revisionist power. To determine India's level of institutionalized cooperation with both status quo and revisionist powers, we must first determine a measure of institutionalized cooperation. To do this, in this chapter, we will discuss treaties, treaty networks, and measures of institutionalized cooperation. Finally, we will address the methods and measurements for determining whether India is a status quo or a revisionist power.

Cooperation

International relations has often examined the global order as being one in which states are the fundamental actors. This is important, as it means that fundamentally the global order is a self-help system. In other words, states are responsible for their own actions and their own security. One important debate in international relations is why states would choose to cooperate in the first place. If indeed the world is a self-help system, and states can only rely on themselves to provide for their own security, then why would they cooperate with other states, which might in turn bolster the security of other states while negatively affecting one's own state security. Realists focus on the fact that the world system is anarchic, meaning that there is no world government that controls the behavior of states. In other words, there is nothing requiring other states to help to provide security to any other states in the global system. Specifically, they see global anarchy as creating a zero-sum game between states: if a state gains any power, other states will lose power. In other words, power is finite, and all of it is relative. States are always gaining and losing power vis-à-vis other states in the system. What this creates is an intense competition between states, where even issues on which two states can cooperate can lead to both states being wary of cooperation out of fear that the other state will gain more power relative to the given state. Each state looks to maximize its own power interests while trying to minimize the amount of power that any other state could gain through the interaction (Grieco, Powell, and Snidal 1993). The competitive nature of such a zero-sum game is also known as relative gains. Relative gains further typify a zero-sum game in that any interaction between states is viewed as a competition and game where there can only be one state that wins. Relative gains make it not beneficial for a state to cooperate with any other state, even if both states might benefit from that cooperation; each state is worried about the amount that other states benefit in comparison to the amount that the state would benefit by cooperating at all. The scholars who believe strongly in the existence of relative gains are very skeptical about the possibility of institutionalized cooperation between states, and that even though cooperation on individual issues may be possible, it will last only until the power dynamic between the two states shifts. This is a very pessimistic view of states' abilities or desires to cooperate on any issue area. It is important to note that scholars who view the world through this spectrum view every interaction as power-based, and thus all interactions must be examined through an understanding of the changing power dynamics that each interaction brings.

In contrast to scholars who believe in relative gains, other scholars tend to view interactions between states not as a zero-sum game, but rather as a positive-sum game. In other words, states that choose to cooperate can both benefit from the interaction as opposed to one state gaining more power than another state. States do not have to be concerned about the power dynamics of interacting with other states; rather, the states can maximize their own benefit from cooperating, realizing full well that the cooperating state is also benefitting from the interaction (Keohane and Martin 1995; Snidal 1991). Scholars who view interactions from this perspective believe in absolute gains. In other words, rather than being worried about the effect of cooperation on the other state, states can be more driven to cooperate to ensure that the state benefits. It should be noted that scholars who believe in absolute gains do not view every interaction as being power-driven, and often discount the relative power dynamics between states. Interactions between states are able to be mutually beneficial, which allows cooperation between states. Interestingly, while scholars who believe in relative gains consistently argue that cooperation in security matters is very difficult to realize among states, scholars who believe in absolute gains focus on showing that cooperation is possible between states involving trade. Thus, although the two theoretical perspectives seem diametrically opposed to one another, they actually may not be. It could be that cooperation between states is merely more difficult when states are addressing security issues, whereas issues of trade might be much less contentious, and more easily lead to cooperation between states.

Despite the difficulty in overcoming the relative gains problems, states still continue to cooperate on many different issues. They cooperate with other states on issues such as trade and security. Cooperation between states is built through both bilateral (between two states) and multilateral (involving three or more states) relationships. Some scholars have noted that cooperation is easier to achieve through trade than through security because all states involved in trade benefit from cooperation (Keohane 2005). Scholars such as Keohane (2005) have noted that cooperation between states is incredibly important because it creates a long-term relationship that not only benefits the states that are cooperating but also constrains state behavior. States that have built long-term relationships through cooperation are much less likely to resolve disputes with those states through military conflict (Slobodchikoff 2013). Instead, they are much more likely to resolve their disputes through peaceful means and negotiation. It is important to note that power dynamics are important features of cooperation. In power symmetric relationships, it is easier to cooperate as relative equals, whereas in power asymmetric relationships, the stronger power can coerce less powerful states and require cooperation on certain issues such as trade. For example, the Soviet Union's regional hegemonic status forced neighboring Finland to engage in a multifaceted relationship despite the fact that Finland was extremely suspicious of Soviet intentions and wary of Soviet foreign policy (Slobodchikoff 2013; Korhonen 2010).

States must make the determination whether or not they should cooperate with other states. This is not an easy decision, but rather one that must be
made strategically. On the one hand, they may be able to achieve gains that
would normally not be attainable without cooperation. On the other hand,
they must be able to trust that states will adhere to cooperative agreements
and must be wary of how much to cooperate. In situations of power asymmetry, where one state is much more powerful than the other state, the
weaker power must be warier of cooperating due to the ability of the more
powerful state to coerce the weaker state. However, the weaker states also
have more to gain through cooperation than they do by not cooperating.
Therefore, weaker states must be very strategic in the decision making process as to whether or not to cooperate. Cooperation is easier with states that
have shared ideologies. Thus, states are likelier to build cooperative relationships with states that share their own preferences and beliefs than with states
that don't. For example, the United States is much more likely to build a
cooperative relationship with the United Kingdom than with Senegal. We
now turn to a discussion of the actors involved in creating cooperative
relationships.

Actors in Cooperation

International relations scholars have often delineated domestic politics
from international relations. They argue that comparative politics studies
domestic politics, while international relations focuses only on the relationship between states. Thus, they should be considered as separate entities
and should be studied separately (Walt 1985; Waltz 1979). Scholars have
more recently challenged this notion by arguing that domestic politics and
international relations are mutually reinforcing and thus linked (Goldstein
and Gowa 2002; Goldstein 1996; Henisz and Mansfield 2006; Milner
1999; Moravcsik 1997; Putnam 1988). For example, Moravcsik (1997)
argues that internal interest groups fight for dominance over preferences.
When domestic interest groups are able to set the domestic agenda according to their preferences, a state's foreign policy will reflect those preferences.
Thus, the domestic preferences in turn constrain a state's foreign policy.

In contrast to Moravcsik (1997), Putnam (1988) argues that a two-level
game exists between foreign policy and domestic policy. Since policy makers
are beholden to voters and domestic constituencies, they can use foreign
affairs to satisfy their domestic constituencies while at the same time being
constrained in their own foreign policy preferences by domestic constituencies. Moreover, a state's foreign policy preferences can also have a profound

effect on a state's domestic constituencies and their policy preferences. In other words, a feedback loop develops between both levels.

National elites have been known to use international relations and international events to pursue a domestic agenda. One example of this was that President Reagan really wanted to push for trade liberalization. Although a Democratic Congress opposed liberalizing trade, the Reagan administration constructed treaties with Canada that forced Congress to approve free trade between Canada and the United States (Goldstein 1996). When Reagan signed the treaties, he effectively put pressure on Congress to act so that they would not upset their domestic constituencies. Once the United States had signed the treaties, domestic industries were told that protectionist measures could not be used to protect industries due to the requirement to abide by treaty obligations.

In contrast to US domestic industry pushback, the Canadian government was happy to enter into free trade agreements with the United States to limit the preferential treatment of US companies by the US government. The Canadian government worried that Canadian companies would not be able to effectively compete with American companies if American companies received preferential treatment from the US government (Goldstein 1996). Despite the fact that the new treaties with Canada sometimes came into conflict with US preferences, the US has upheld its agreements with Canada. While the Trump administration tried to renegotiate the treaties, the administration has continued to abide by these treaties. The government has chosen to abide by those treaties even when it was not in their best interests to do so. Even though it would have been far better for US businesses and US interests to violate the treaties, the government nevertheless felt constrained by the treaties and agreed to abide by them (Goldstein 1996).

The example of treaties constraining hegemonic behavior is by no means unique. In fact, the United States has often been constrained by international treaties, and despite the fact that it would be more logical to violate the treaties in the short term, the United States has often abided by those treaties. It has done so even when it has not benefited in the short term (Mattli and Büthe 2003). For example, Mattli and Büthe (2003) have argue that the United States has often been at a disadvantage when making agreements with the European Union as well as with individual European countries over standards. These agreements have often put the United States at a disadvantage and yet the United States has agreed to these standards in the hopes that it would lead to future agreements that would be more beneficial to the United States. More importantly, the United States continues to abide by most of those treaties even if it is not in its interests to do so. In other words, international agreements set the stage for future cooperation, and a hegemonic power must have a longer view of a relationship than merely one or two agreements. The hegemon must gamble that a specific agreement, even if it is not to the hegemon's advantage, may lead to future agreements that are, and in the long term the hegemon will benefit tremendously from the overall relationship.

It is generally accepted that hegemonic states will not allow themselves to be constrained by agreements. In fact, this argument runs counter to many realist arguments against the effectiveness of treaties. Downs, Rocke, and Barsoom (1996) argue that the reason there is such a high rate of compliance with international agreements is because the most powerful countries want to comply with those treaties. In other words, if powerful states did not want to comply with a treaty, they wouldn't. Instead, they would either renegotiate the treaty or just ignore the treaty in the first place. In the case of multilateral treaties, powerful states would try to convince other states not to comply with a treaty and thus render the treaty moot.

One example of this was during George W. Bush's administration when the United States tried to get other states to agree to sign bilateral nonsurrender agreements, where those states would never turn over American soldiers to the International Criminal Courts (Kelley 2007). According to Kelley (2007), Washington was unhappy with the fact that American soldiers could be tried by international courts, rendering the US ineffective at protecting its own military. Thus, it pressured other states to sign these nonsurrender agreements but ultimately was forced to abandon its pressure as most of the states refused to sign the nonsurrender agreements. Ultimately, Kelley (2007) finds that even with extreme hegemonic pressure, international agreements are not only abided by, they are also likely to constrain the behaviors of other states that do not wish to adhere to the original agreement. International agreements are considered extremely important, and even if they can be violated, the repercussions for doing so are often very expensive as states will refuse to enter into future agreements with those states that often violate previously signed agreements.

Design Features of Bilateral Relations

It is important to note that strong and weak states both believe that cooperation is in their best interest. However, the fact that it may be in their best interest does not ensure their cooperation. There are myriads of obstacles to cooperation. One of the major obstacles to cooperation is mistrust. Weaker states are very concerned with the fact that they cannot trust stronger states to abide by agreements. After all, there is nothing preventing a stronger state from only cooperating when it is in the interest of the stronger state, but as soon as it is no longer in the interest of the stronger state to cooperate it can cease to do so. There is very little that a weaker state can do to prevent a stronger state from violating previous agreements. Weaker states are also concerned with power asymmetry and the inability of weaker states to enforce agreements. Despite these obstacles, weaker states can use legalization and treaty nesting as ways to combat mistrust and power asymmetry (Slobodchikoff 2013).

Legalization of treaties and agreements is a very important strategy by states to try to constrain states from violating the agreements. The strategy of legalization of treaties and the use of laws to govern the interaction between states has seen a large rise in usage by states since the 1990s (Goldstein et al. 2000). Legalization is a type of institutionalization. Specifically, legalization has three basic components. Obligation means that states are bound by rules and international law. Precision means that international rules clearly and unambiguously define and lay out rules of conduct for states to abide by. Delegation is the ability of states to appoint arbiters, resolve disputes, and make further rules (Abbott et al. 2000, 401).

Many relations between states are characterized by mistrust. It is often very difficult, especially in the beginning stages of a relationship, to trust another state to abide by its agreements and not violate them. Thus, states must first begin to cooperate on agreements that are mutually beneficial and relatively easy to accomplish. As states fulfill their obligations and adhere to prior agreements, states can begin to slowly build trust. In other words, states must begin to cooperate and by proving their ability to abide by agreements, they build trust with other states (Kydd 2000, 2001). Interestingly, as states begin to develop more complex agreements and agreements on more complex issues, they often choose to further legalize new agreements. One of the methods of doing this is through treaty nesting where a treaty specifically references a prior treaty, which reinforces both treaties and makes it more difficult to violate those treaties. If one of the treaties that is nested within a previous treaty is violated, then both treaties are violated. This raises the cost to a state of violating a given treaty that is nested within other treaties (Slobodchikoff 2013). In other words, in addition to legalization, states often turn to other design features such as treaty nesting to overcome mistrust and lack of cooperation. Treaty nesting is a specific strategy that is used by states to tie different treaties together by specifically citing prior treaties in new treaties, which makes both treaties stronger (Willerton, Slobodchikoff, and Goertz 2012; Willerton, Goertz, and Slobodchikoff 2015).

Both legalization and treaty nesting are extremely important in overcoming both mistrust and power asymmetry in relationships. However, both of these design features require the use of treaties. Legalization refers to the constraints and the requirements of individual treaties upon the signatories of the treaty, while treaty nesting refers to the actual links between the treaties themselves. It is important, however, to understand the basic aspects of treaties and agreements themselves to further illustrate the methods that are used to overcome constraints to cooperation.

Treaties and Agreements

States will tend to cooperate only if it is in their best interest to do so. It is very difficult to force states to cooperate if they do not want to. States are rational actors and thus are not likely to violate their own interests and cooperate if it would not be in their interest to cooperate. As former Finnish foreign minister Keijo Korhonen once stated, "Even the most powerful state in the world cannot protect all of its citizens without the help of other states; cooperation is a necessity for all states who wish to have an international presence" (Korhonen 2010).

It is important to note that treaties and agreements need to be clearly defined before any analysis is undertaken. What types of agreements should be used to analyze a relationship clearly? In terms of international law, treaties refer to any legally binding written agreements between states (Carter, Trimble, and Weiner 2007; Sinclair 1984). The Vienna Convention on the Law of Treaties establishes a comprehensive list of rules on treaty construction, interpretation, and termination. States can also sign other agreements such as memoranda of understanding and joint press releases, which, while not legally binding, are often indicators of the level of cooperation between states.

Due to the fact that treaties and agreements are legally binding, it is natural to wonder why states would enter into an agreement or treaty in the first place. After all, entering into a treaty and agreement constrains a state's future behavior. However, it is precisely because it is constraining that both sides would want to enter into such an agreement. Entering into such agreements and then violating them will prove a state's untrustworthiness and limit future cooperation. It is often better for states to abide by treaties so that future treaties and agreements may be more beneficial even if current agreements and treaties are not. Moreover, certain treaties and agreements possess dispute settlement mechanisms that can help when there is a dispute between signatories. Many modern treaties are specifically designed to have dispute settlement mechanisms and to be in force for a finite length of time to ensure cooperation and ultimately force the signatories to abide by the provisions of the agreements and treaties.

It should be noted that treaties and agreements are negotiated. This means that negotiators will specifically argue over the correct wording of a treaty or agreement. Language matters and specific word usage matters. Thus, it's extremely important, especially for weaker states, to ensure that the words agreed to in a treaty will not bind them in ways that are unacceptable. Ultimately, legally binding treaties and the use of treaty nesting establish a set of rules for cooperation between states as well as an acceptance by states of specific rules established by global powers. The global hegemon is responsible for creating order and other states must choose whether or not to abide by that global order (Slobodchikoff 2014). States that use treaty nesting within an established order are more likely to work to protect that order than they are to challenge that order. In other words, states that have higher levels of institutionalized cooperation with hegemonic powers are status quo powers. If they have higher levels of institutionalized cooperation with revisionist powers, then that state could be considered to be revisionist.

Treaties establish a set of rules for cooperation between states within a global order. They are a necessary component of international relations by which both strong and weak states must abide if they are to be able to continue to cooperate with other states. For weak states, treaties provide protection from stronger states, while still providing the opportunity to cooperate with stronger states. One example of this was in 1948 when the Soviet Union insisted on negotiating a friendship treaty with Finland. Moscow wanted to both station Soviet troops in Finland and to make Finland a satellite state much like Hungary and Romania. Due to the power asymmetry between Finland and the Soviet Union, the Finns realized that they had no choice but to cooperate with the Soviet Union. However, they also realized that they could ensure that the language in the treaty was acceptable to them and help guide the relationship between the Soviet Union and Finland. Thus, the Finns insisted on using specific language in the treaty with the Soviet Union to ensure that they would not become a satellite state of the Soviet Union (Korhonen 2010). The Soviet Union was stretched thin following World War II, and could not just send troops to invade Finland. Therefore, if Moscow wanted to station troops in Finland, it had to get Helsinki to agree to allow those troops through the treaty of cooperation.

Treaties establish a pattern of behavior on which other states rely and violating treaties creates a large reputational cost. Often treaties are the result of negotiated compromise. For example, the friendship treaty between the Soviet Union and Finland signed in 1948 included a lot of compromise on the specific wording of the treaty. Specifically, the Finns insisted upon specific wording that stated that Moscow would only send troops to Finland should the Finns not be able to defend themselves. The importance of the wording meant that the Finns could keep out Soviet troops while stating to the Soviet Union that Soviet troops would be welcome if Finland was about to be invaded by Western troops. The Finns argued that they could protect themselves but would be quick to call upon aid from Moscow should it become necessary. As this example shows, Finland, a weaker state, was able to insist upon specific language that protected the Finns from becoming a satellite state. Moscow, on the other hand, was willing to adopt specific language in the treaty as a conciliatory gesture due to the fact that it was extremely important for Moscow to have the treaty in the first place. Thus, it should be kept in mind that weaker states often play a very important role in developing treaties and receive gains that are more than they would receive based upon their relative power capabilities.

While it is easy to focus on the importance of a single treaty, each individual treaty is not created in a vacuum. Each subsequent treaty is at least somewhat influenced by previous treaties as well as the relationship between the signatories. This is even more accurate when examining treaty nestedness, because the treaties themselves state the relationship between previous treaties and the treaty that is nested within them. In other words, an individual treaty is a single attempt at cooperation. Nested treaties, on the other hand, show the institutionalization of treaties. In fact, the more nesting that occurs in a relationship, the more institutionalized the relationship, and thus the more difficult it is to destroy the relationship through conflict (Slobodchikoff 2013). We now turn to a discussion of treaty nesting, treaty architecture, and building relationships.

Treaty Nesting

Prior work on treaty nesting has focused on examining how treaties interact with one another. Specifically, the idea is that since treaties are negotiated, each treaty is not totally separate from previous treaties that have been negotiated. Further, since treaties are the building blocks of a relationship, each treaty provides a foundation for a relationship. The earliest studies of treaty nesting used nesting to provide more of a qualitative analysis of specific treaties in the bilateral relationship between states given high levels of mistrust. Specifically, Willerton, Slobodchikoff, and Goertz (2012) focused on examining the bilateral relationships between Russia and Turkmenistan and between Russia and Georgia to see how nesting was used to overcome mistrust. Using network analysis, Willerton, Slobodchikoff, and Goertz (2012) examined the architecture of the bilateral relationship. Creating a hypothetical example, we demonstrate how treaty architecture is shown (see fig. 4).

In figure 4, Treaty A is nested in both Treaty B and Treaty C. In other words, both Treaty B and Treaty C specifically mention Treaty A within the respective treaties. However, Treaty B is not nested in Treaty C. There is no tie between them. Further, as figure 4 shows, Treaty A is a central treaty in the relationship between Treaty A, Treaty B, and Treaty C. We have set the node (Treaty A) to its degree centrality score. This is why the node of Treaty A is larger than Treaty B and Treaty C. Figure 4 begins to show the treaty architecture, with Treaty A being the most central treaty and thus the most important treaty in the relationship. In figure 5, each of the treaties is nested in the other two treaties (see fig. 5). In other words, there is no single treaty that is central to the relationship. Rather, all of the treaties have equal centrality scores. Thus, the treaty architecture is slightly different.

Slobodchikoff (2013) built upon the work by Willerton, Slobodchikoff, and Goertz (2012). He examined Russia's relationship with each of the former Soviet states excluding the Baltic states. He built upon the fact that by using network analysis to examine treaties, scholars would be able to see the architecture of a bilateral relationship. Using treaty network analysis, he was able to show which treaties were the most central in a relationship. These treaties were the lodestone treaties, and were the most important in the bilateral relationship. Further, he was able to show how treaties were tied to each other. He built upon the idea that an individual treaty is an attempt at cooperation while nested treaties are attempts at institutionalizing the relationship.

Slobodchikoff (2013) speculates that the more the treaties are tied to one another, the more stable the cooperative relationship. For example, figure 6 shows an ad hoc relationship between India and South Africa (see fig. 6). Several treaties are tied to each other, but there seems to be more of an ad hoc relationship since there are several different subnetworks that are not tied together. In other words, there is some cooperation, but the cooperation is specific to certain issue areas and does not possess institutionalized cooperation. In contrast, figure 7 shows a relationship that seems to be less ad hoc and more institutionalized (see fig. 7). It shows the relationship between India and the EU as a supranational organization. It indicates that there is

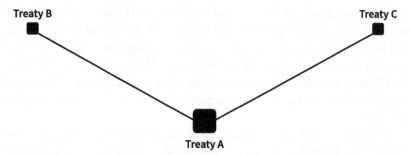

Fig. 4. Treaty Nesting

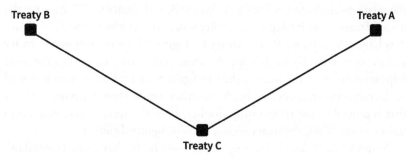

Fig. 5. Treaty Network

much more institutionalization in the relationship, especially in the subnetwork located on the left-hand side of the figure.

To determine the quality of a relationship, Slobodchikoff (2013) developed a new measure of a cooperative relationship between two states as being the number of treaty ties divided by the total number of treaties. Using this measure over time, he was able to determine the quality of institutionalization of the bilateral relationship. Let's examine a hypothetical relationship between two states (see table 3). As table 3 shows, in each decade of the relationship, the two states sign five treaties. Since treaties are cumulative, the total number of treaties would be the number of treaties signed in a specific decade plus all of those signed in the preceding decades. Further, the number of ties also increases in the same way. The measure of institutionalized cooperation in a given decade is the total number of ties up to that given decade divided by the total number of treaties signed over that same period of time. It is incredibly important that the exact same time period be examined when comparing institutionalized cooperation scores. More specifically, there should be a specific time (T0) from which the measurement occurs to ensure that appropriate comparisons can be made. In our analysis, we are specifically

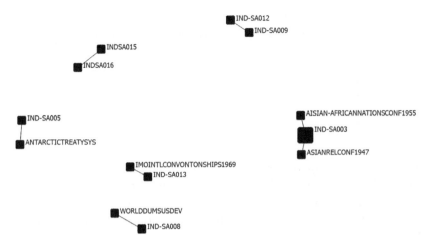

Fig. 6. India–South Africa Treaty Network

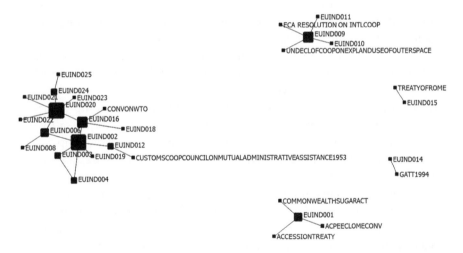

Fig. 7. India-EU Treaty Network

interested in the post–Cold War period as after the end of the Cold War is the time in which unipolarity and the United States' supremacy begins. Thus, all of our comparisons begin after the end of the Cold War. While we understand that there was a relationship between the states examined prior to the end of the Cold War, beginning our analysis at the end of the Cold War is the best way to be able to compare the quality of bilateral relationships.

It is important to establish a baseline for determining the quality of a

Table 3. Institutionalized Cooperation Score

Years	N Treaties	N Ties	Cooperation Score
1980s	5	1	.2
1990s	5	3	.4
2000s	5	8	.8
2010s	5	10	1.1
Totals	**20**	**22**	**1.1**

bilateral relationship. A measure of less than 1 indicated a relationship that was ad hoc. In other words, there were attempts at cooperating but few attempts at institutionalizing that cooperation. A measure greater than 1 indicated that there was institutionalized cooperation (see table 4). Table 4 shows the different classifications of the quality of the bilateral relationship. Again, if the number of treaty ties divided by the number of treaties signed exceeds 1, the relationship is a cooperative one. If the number of treaty ties divided by the number of treaties signed is equal to 1, the relationship is on the brink of institutionalized cooperation. If the number of treaty ties divided by the number of treaties signed is less than 1, then it indicates an ad hoc relationship. This does not mean that there is no relationship, but that there has been little effort toward institutionalizing the relationship. An ad hoc relationship can occur because there is really no need to develop a long-term institutionalized relationship. Often, an ad hoc relationship occurs either at the very beginning of a relationship or if there are only one or two issue areas that require cooperation. Similarly, an ad hoc relationship can develop if either one of the states deeply mistrusts the other state and only wants very limited cooperation.

Finally, Slobodchikoff (2013) showed that the higher the institutionalized cooperation score, the less likely there is to be conflict between the two states. In other words, the more institutionalized the cooperation, the more likely there is to be peaceful relations between the states and the better the bilateral relationship.

Treaty nesting as a tool in building bilateral and multilateral relationships is not unique to the post-Soviet region. Scholars have used treaty nesting and treaty networks to study the quality of the relationships between China and Russia (Ambrosio 2017) and China and the European Union (Slobodchikoff 2017a). Further, treaty networks have been used to study the quality of relationships between states and de facto states (Ambrosio and Lange 2016).

In South Asia, treaty networks have been used to study the quality of the

Table 4. Measure of Cooperative Relationship

Cooperative Relationship	Ties/Treaties > 1
Neutral Relationship	Ties/Treaties = 1
Ad hoc Relationship	Ties/Treaties < 1

relationship between India and Russia (Slobodchikoff and Tandon 2017) and India and Pakistan (Tandon and Slobodchikoff 2019; Slobodchikoff and Tandon 2019). Specifically, Tandon and Slobodchikoff (2019) show how India and Pakistan are able to build a relationship through treaty networks despite the fact that both states are rivals. While India and Pakistan remain rivals, they argue that both states have been able to build some trust over time and, through the use of treaty nesting, have decreased the likelihood of a major militarized conflict between the two states.

Treaty networks are not only important tools to understanding a bilateral relationship between states, they can also be useful in showing the hierarchical structure of global and regional order and show how involved a given state is within the global or regional order. For example, Slobodchikoff (2014) shows how Russia was able to establish a regional order using treaty nesting. Moscow used both bilateral and multilateral treaties to establish and secure the regional order. He argues that the states that accepted the regional order were more willing to engage with Russia to get benefits provided by the hegemon. In exchange for the benefits provided by the regional hegemon, the states agreed to abide by the rules established by the great power. Slobodchikoff and Aleprete (2020) further showed that Russia's attempts to create a regional order and integrate the post-Soviet space were effective in that the states that were most committed to the regional order were more likely to align themselves politically with Moscow.

It is important to note that treaty networks are able to illustrate regional and global order. States that align themselves within the regional order are more likely to institutionalize their cooperation with the great powers of that order (Slobodchikoff 2014). In the case of the Russian regional order, Kazakhstan, Armenia, and Belarus were the most willing to try to integrate fully within the regional order while Georgia was the least willing. That did not mean that there was no cooperation with Georgia, merely that Moscow and Tbilisi had a much more ad hoc level of cooperation, cooperating when necessary but not working to institutionalize cooperation. We now turn to a discussion of the global order in South Asia, and the importance of India to that global order.

India's Place in the Global Order

The end of World War II ushered in a new era of bipolarity. Both the United States and the Soviet Union began a new era of competition with each state trying to woo other states into joining into an alliance with them. This was a global competition by both powers to try to not only increase their own power but also to decrease the power of their adversary. In South Asia, both the Soviet Union and the United States tried to gain the support of the regional great powers. Pakistan allied itself with the United States while India allied itself more with the Soviet Union. In keeping an arms race between the two superpowers going, the United States sold arms to Pakistan while the Soviet Union sold arms to India. In this way, both India and Pakistan were able to keep up their regional rivalry by becoming players in the global rivalry. In other words, the regional rivalry mirrored the global rivalry.

India and Pakistan fought over Kashmir and used the arms bought from their benefactors against each other. Once both states gained nuclear weapons, their regional rivalry became even more important to the global hierarchy. A war between the two states would threaten to bring in both the Soviet Union and the United States into a regional conflict and have profound implications for stability in the region and around the world. Despite the fact that the rivalry occasionally heated up, it did not force the coalition partners into a larger conflict.

In 1991, the Soviet Union ceased to exist and a bipolar world order became unipolar. Moscow tried to retain its trade ties with India especially through the sales of arms. Washington, on the other hand, sensed a new market and tried to improve ties with India. However, Washington also had to be cognizant that it did not want to hurt its relationship with Pakistan. Therefore, Washington cautiously tried to improve relations with New Delhi. Instead of competing ideologically and continuing the Cold War, Moscow and Washington renewed a competition for economic gains especially in the defense industry. However, Washington did not believe that it needed New Delhi to maintain its unipolarity. In fact, Washington believed that the era of geopolitics and competition over the global order had been won. In other words, Washington did not need to ask for support from New Delhi; rather, that support would be a given.

Following September 11, 2001, Washington developed the idea that either you were with us or you were against us. They didn't need to compete with rivals or aid their allies; rather, the allies needed to show their support for Washington and its foreign policy. Pakistan began to gain increased importance during the subsequent war on terror, and New Delhi was no longer of any strategic importance to Washington and the maintenance of the unipolar system. All of Washington's attention was focused on first Afghanistan and then Iraq. There was very little room for strategic thinking and for a long-term foreign policy that would need the support of New Delhi.

China's rapid rise in power in the latter part of the first decade of the 21st century was a concern for Washington, and President Obama declared a pivot to Asia in terms of a strategic shift in foreign policy. Obama stated that for too long US foreign policy had been focused on Europe, and that it was a time for a fundamental shift away from a Eurocentric foreign policy towards a more Asia-centered foreign policy. He recognized that this was necessary to compete with China and to try to maintain supremacy in Asia. However, it was more difficult to achieve this shift than to state it. In fact, there was actually very little shift in terms of subsequent substantive agreements between Washington and New Delhi (Slobodchikoff and Tandon 2017). Moscow continued to dominate the military defense industry in its agreements with New Delhi. However, New Delhi officially remained neutral and insisted that it would not be exclusive in its agreements. In fact, New Delhi stated that it welcomed a better relationship with Washington while not sacrificing its relationship with Moscow.

Starting in 2007 at the Munich security conference, Russian president Vladimir Putin outlined a growing list of complaints with the United States as the global hegemon. For the first time, he publicly stated that it was time to move from a unipolar system to a multipolar system and that Russia, while not directly opposing the United States, would aid in helping a transition from unipolarity to multipolarity. Putin argued that it was time for the United States to take into account the ideas and the positions of other countries and to stop acting as though Washington's opinion was the only one that mattered. In other words, Putin was tired of not being taken seriously and not having a seat at the table when it came to strategic interests that affected the whole world. He believed that Moscow deserved to play an important role as a great power and that the US should not be so dismissive of other countries and their strategic interests. He stipulated that the US discounted Russia as being merely a regional power and thus not important when decisions affecting the international community were taken. Putin perceived this as arrogance on the part of the United States and at that point began to challenge the global order established by the United States.

In 2008, Moscow invaded Georgia in an effort to maintain its regional sphere of influence and to ensure that NATO would not spread by accepting Georgia as a member state. Washington was very surprised by Moscow's actions. However, Putin was indicating that he had his own form of the

Monroe Doctrine. He was drawing a line and stating that he would not allow NATO expansion into any of the former Soviet states with the exception of the Baltic states, which had already joined.

In 2013, Putin again surprised the West by supporting an insurrection in southeast Ukraine to ensure that Ukraine would not be able to join NATO or the EU. Again, he was indicating his policy of the Monroe Doctrine applied to the former Soviet Union. Both the invasion of Georgia and Russian actions in Ukraine showed Russia's willingness to challenge Washington's supremacy and begin to challenge the global order.

During this period of time, China was also beginning to challenge the global order. However, it was doing so in a subtler way. It began to develop economic initiatives as a contrast to Washington's liberal order. States were given options to receive loans from the Chinese government without any requirements to develop liberal policies and democratic governance. Getting such loans is especially attractive to states in Central Asia that are more authoritarian in nature and are not happy with adopting liberal reforms. China provided an attractive alternative for those states. In fact, Beijing's early efforts at providing an alternative to the liberal global order later led to the development of the One Belt One Road policy.

States such as Brazil, Russia, India, China, and South Africa (BRICS) and others have long desired a multipolar global order, where they have a larger say in shaping global affairs. International relations scholars have debated whether or not the current system is unipolar with the United States acting as a global hegemon. In terms of military power, the United States maintains its global dominance, far outspending its rivals and competitors, thus maintaining the largest and most well-equipped armed forces in the world. While the US remains the world's largest economy, it continues to face growing competition from rising powers like China, India, and entities such as the European Union. Increasingly, the United States has been unwilling as well as unable to handle global crises, both economic and security related. It has been unable to thwart North Korea's nuclear proliferation. It has been unable to entirely eliminate the Islamic State and other extremist fundamentalist groups. It has been a reluctant participant in the Syrian civil war, allowing states like Russia and Turkey to take the lead in shaping the situation on the ground. These events point to the United States' lack of global leadership. It can be argued that we are witnessing the transition of global order toward a multipolar system, where a group of major powers jointly govern and shape the rules of the system, under which other states must operate.

According to General Michael Hayden, the former director of both the Central Intelligence Agency and the National Security Agency, the global order is currently at an inflection point. The challenge against the liberal order is strong enough that it is far from clear whether the liberal order will survive (Hayden 2018). The only way that the liberal order can survive is if enough regional great powers are committed to maintain that order. Specifically, the regional great powers must have institutionalized relationships with those states that are allied and committed to maintain the global order.

Although China and Russia were in favor of a multipolar system, neither could directly challenge US power. Russia and China also recognized the importance of gaining India as a valuable ally in countering American hegemony.[2] Beginning in 2002, the leaders of Russia, China and India have held annual summits to increase cooperation between themselves. The tripartite meetings in 2017 reiterated that all three states were interested in creating a global system based on international law and moving toward a multipolar system. With the rise of right-wing nationalism in India under the Narendra Modi administration, the three countries may find themselves more aligned than ever before in terms of their worldview. While India prefers the status quo, it also has a strong preference for multilateralism. India prefers noninterventionism in the domestic affairs of other states. When intervention is carried out, India has supported a multilateral coalition versus unilateral actions by powerful states. On the other hand, the United States has increasingly preferred a unilateral course of action in international affairs, sometimes in violation of international law.

While India was officially nonaligned during the Cold War, it maintained a close friendship with the Soviet Union. India's relations with the United States have been much more turbulent, especially after India's entry into the nuclear power states club. The United States' close ties with Pakistan, including the provision of military and monetary aid, had further worsened Indo-American ties. In the last few decades, India has faced rapid economic growth and has enhanced its military power. It is also situated strategically to counter China's rising aggression and territorial expansion. The United States realized that it needed India as an important ally to prevent China and Russia from developing sufficient power and ability to challenge the unipolar system. Relations between the two started to improve during the Bush administration and continued to steadily improve during the subsequent

---

2. http://www.scmp.com/comment/insight-opinion/article/2124329/russia-india-china-meeting-shows-multipolar-world-order

Obama and Trump administrations. Today, the United States and India have developed a much closer relation in an effort to balance the rise of China's power as well as to counter rising Chinese aggression in the Asia Pacific. While there are points of cooperation and conflict in each of the above bilateral relationships, India continues to preserve a balance by maintaining close ties with both Russia and the United States. Despite several military confrontations and border skirmishes along the disputed territory, India and China also continue to maintain cooperative ties, especially in the economic domain. This further complicates the future of the current global order.

While Russia and China are indeed dissatisfied states in the current global order, India is still in play for both the United States on one side and Russia and China on the other. Indeed, it has become the lynchpin in determining the future of the global system. We argue that a regional great power state like India can serve as a lynchpin in this transition from unipolarity toward multipolarity. By choosing to side with Russia and China instead of the United States and the European Union, India can act as a catalyst in a global transition of power. Current trends point to increasing cooperation between India and the United States. As the world's largest and leading democracies, they have much in common with each other. It is widely expected that they will continue to cooperate economically, and India will be crucial ally in the United States' "pivot to" or "rebalancing in" Asia. India and the United States share a common concern for the rise of China and its expanding aggression in the Asia-Pacific as well as globally. Much has been written about the close ties developed between Modi and the Obama administration. Modi and Trump also got off to a good start at their first meeting in June 2017 and the close economic, security, and political cooperation between the two countries is expected to continue. The successful Indian diaspora in the United States provides a crucial connection between the two states. These trends suggest that India is being pulled away from the Russian sphere of influence by the United States and is realigning its foreign policy interests with the United States. We now turn to a discussion on the methodology of determining India's place in the global order.

Measuring India's Place in the Global Order

Using the level of bilateral cooperation measure developed by Slobodchikoff (2013), we can determine the quality of the relationships between India and other countries. Further, since we know that the creation and maintenance of the global order uses treaty nesting and treaty networks to institutionalize the global order, it is possible to place a state within the global order. In other words, if a state has institutionalized its relationships with the great powers of the global order, then that state is vested within the global order. With the US being the supreme power as the global hegemon, the US has created the current liberal order. We can determine how vested in the global order India is by examining the bilateral relationship between India and the United States. However, we need to examine more than just the relationship between India and the United States. We also need to examine the relationship between India and the other great powers in the global order. These major powers work to maintain the global order established by the United States. These powers include the United Kingdom, France, Germany, and the EU as a whole as well as Japan, which is a major regional power. Looking at each of the relationships between India and each of those states or organizations allows us to determine how committed India is to the current global order.

If India is not a status quo power but rather a revisionist power, then we should see evidence that India has more of an institutionalized relationship with great powers that are challenging the global order. The revisionist great powers include Russia, China, and Iran. In other words, we need to create specific categories in which we can place India that would allow us to accurately determine whether India is a status quo power or a revisionist power. Those categories are a solid status quo power, a leaning status quo power, an undecided power, a leaning revisionist power, or a solid revisionist power (see table 5). We will now discuss each of these categories separately.

Solid Status Quo Power

To be a solid status quo power, a state must be allied with the other solid status quo powers. To be termed a status quo power, the state must believe in the ideology of the global order and be dedicated to maintaining the status quo. As table 4 shows, if India is to be categorized as a solid status quo power then it must develop an institutionalized cooperative relationship with the global hegemon, the United States. However, merely having an institutionalized cooperative relationship with the global hegemon is not enough to be considered a solid status quo power. In addition, a solid status quo power should also have institutionalized cooperative relationships with the other major powers of the current global order. In other words, if India were to be considered a solid status quo power, it should have an insti-

Table 5. Categorization of Status Quo vs. Revisionist Power

Solid Status Quo	Leans Status Quo	Undecided	Leans Revisionist	Solid Revisionist
Institutionalized Cooperative Relationship with US	Institutionalized Cooperative Relationship with US	Either no institutionalized cooperative relationships **OR** Institutionalized Cooperative Relationship with both the United States (major status quo power) and Russia (major revisionist power)	Institutionalized Cooperative Relationship with Russia	Institutionalized Cooperative Relationship with Russia
Institutionalized Cooperative Relationship with UK	Ad hoc or Institutionalized Relationship with EU		Ad hoc or Institutionalized Relationship with China	Institutionalized Cooperative Relationship with China
Institutionalized Cooperative Relationship with France	Ad hoc or Institutionalized Relationship with France _or_ Germany		Lacks Institutionalized Cooperative Relationship with US	
Institutionalized Cooperative Relationship with Germany	Ad hoc or Institutionalized Relationship with Japan			
Institutionalized Cooperative Relationship with EU				
Institutionalized Cooperative Relationship with Japan				
Lacks Institutionalized Cooperative Relationship with Russia				

tutionalized cooperative relationship with the United Kingdom, France, Germany, and the EU as a whole. While France and Germany are solid members of the EU, nevertheless they also conduct their own security and defense policies along with their own foreign policies related to trade. Thus, it is important to look at the relationship between the individual states with India as well as with the EU as an entity with India. It is important to note that being classified as a status quo great power does not preclude institutionalized cooperation between a revisionist state and the status quo power. The status quo power may develop an institutionalized cooperative relationship with a revisionist power and yet maintain its true focus on the maintenance and alliance between the states of the current global order.

Leaning Status Quo Power

For a state to be a leaning status quo power it must possess an institutionalized cooperative relationship with the global hegemon. In addition to this, a leaning status quo power will also attempt to develop cooperative relationships with other status quo major powers in the international system. The level of cooperation between a leaning status quo power and other major status quo powers may not be institutionalized; this is the distinguishing criterion between a solid status quo power and a leaning status quo power. Thus, in order to be termed a leaning status quo power, India must develop cooperative relationships with France, the United Kingdom, Germany, and Japan, in addition to demonstrating institutionalized cooperation with the United States. Table 4 shows that the leaning status quo power must both have an institutionalized cooperative relationship with the global hegemon and a cooperative relationship with the other status quo great powers in the global order.

Undecided

An undecided power does not feel strongly about aligning itself with either the status quo powers or the revisionist powers. Therefore, as table 5 shows, an undecided great power may either lack institutionalized cooperative relationships with both the status quo powers or the revisionist powers, or it may choose to develop institutionalized cooperative relationships with both the status quo and revisionist powers. In other words, the great power is not making a specific choice to either support the status quo or revisionist powers. Instead, it is like a free agent that can choose to either develop no relationship whatsoever or develop relationships with both sides.

Leans Revisionist

Contrary to status quo powers, a power that leans revisionist will believe ideologically in the necessity of changing the current status quo. The question of how dedicated a state is to changing the status quo is a matter of degree. As table 5 shows, a great power that leans revisionist should at the very least have an institutionalized cooperative relationship with Russia, one of the most vocal revisionist powers. The state should also have a cooperative relationship with the other main revisionist power, China. Also, any great power that leans revisionist would need to not have an institutionalized cooperative relationship with the United States. This is due to the fact that revisionist powers by definition want to change the global order.

Solid Revisionist Power

A solid revisionist power is again by definition a powerful state that wishes to bring about a change in the global order. However, a solid revisionist power is much more active in trying to bring about that change than a leaning revisionist power. Examples of solid revisionist powers are Russia and China. As table 5 shows, to be considered a solid revisionist power, a great power should have an institutionalized cooperative relationship with both China and Russia as well as have an institutionalized cooperative relationship with other revisionist states such as Iran.

Ultimately, if revisionist powers truly want to bring about change in the global order, they will need to convince other great regional powers. India is not the only such power, but India is an important regional power in South Asia and a key to balancing China's power in Asia as a whole. That is why it is so important to determine whether India is indeed wedded to the current status quo or if it is a revisionist power that will aid Russia and China in developing a multipolar system. India is truly a lynchpin in the struggle to either maintain or create a new global order. In the following sections, we will first look at India's relationships with the status quo powers. In the next chapter we will specifically look at India's relationship with the United States. We will also examine India's relationships with the United Kingdom, France, Germany, and the EU. These are the major states, along with the United

States, upholding the current international order. After we have examined India's relationships with the status quo powers, we will then turn to an examination of India's relationships with revisionist powers. We will especially focus on India's relationships with Russia, China, and Iran. Finally, by comparing all of those relationships, we should be able to make a final determination about whether India is a status quo or a revisionist power and thus the implications for the global order as a whole.

Part 2 • India's Relationship with Status Quo Powers

4 • India-US Relations

United States foreign policy has often been a contest between isolationism and interventionism. From the time of George Washington's farewell address as president, where he cautioned the United States to avoid foreign entanglements, there has been a significant portion of policy makers who have wanted to avoid alliances and interventionism. These policy makers have consistently tried to focus on domestic policy to the exclusion of foreign policy. For example, the United States was slow to enter both World War I and World War II.

After World War II however, the United States realized the importance of developing and maintaining international alliances. From the ashes of World War II, two great powers emerged: the United States and the Soviet Union. World War II had effectively destroyed the other great powers' ability to build an international order. In other words, the post–World War II era created a period of bipolarity in which the United States created a postwar order in the West, while the Soviet Union spread communism and developed its own regional order in Eastern Europe and Asia.

A new era of competition emerged between the United States and the Soviet Union to spread and expand each of their regional orders. Moreover, both states worked to prevent their opponent's world order from growing. This new era of competition was known as the Cold War and it was marked by intense competition between the two states in gaining international allies in various regions around the world. The Cold War spread from Europe to Asia to the Americas to Africa. Very few regions were not affected by this competition.

In South Asia, both the Soviet Union and the United States worked to outcompete each other by recruiting more regional allies. While the United States became closer to Pakistan, the Soviet Union developed a close relationship with India. Moscow's ties to New Delhi were troublesome for the United States, but the United States really worked to ensure its ties with Islamabad.

The end of the Cold War brought new opportunities for US foreign policy. Both Presidents George H. W. Bush and William Clinton realized the importance of the United States being the sole superpower as well as the importance of the shift from bipolarity to unipolarity. Both of them argued that the United States had won the Cold War and that the liberal order had triumphed over communism and the Eastern Bloc. The collapse of the Soviet Union further provided impetus for the United States to look out for its own interests and grow its power further vis-à-vis the other states in the global order. Clinton especially believed that the US economy was a global one, and looked for new ways to open new markets. Additionally, Clinton believed that NATO should expand because not only was NATO's chief mission over, but this was an act that would be relatively low cost in terms of security guarantees for the United States. While Moscow argued that the US had promised not to expand NATO, there was really nothing that Moscow could do to prevent this expansion from taking place.

In response to the Clinton administration's global expansion and increased interventionism, the George W. Bush administration initially tried to retreat and impose a new era of isolationism. During the campaign for president, Bush said that he was not into nation-building and instead wanted to focus on domestic policy. He argued that the United States had won the Cold War and that it was now time to focus inward rather than outward.

The terrorist attacks on September 11, 2001 made Bush pivot from a more isolationist president to one of the most interventionist presidents in the history of the United States. Bush began to use the military to pursue terrorists abroad and believed very strongly in the conviction that either states had to support the United States or that they were against the United States. Nuance was not a part of this new strategy. However, the Bush administration did see the importance of alliances and especially regional alliances in the regions where there was a lot of terrorist activity. Thus, the United States worked very hard to strengthen the relationship between Washington and Islamabad in an attempt to have Pakistan help the United States in the war on terror broadly, but more specifically in the war in Afghanistan against the Taliban. New Delhi was not a priority for Washington during this period; while it was not ignored, relations with Islamabad were deemed to be more strategically important than those with New Delhi.

During the Obama administration, there was a renewed effort to reach out to traditional allies and nontraditional allies in an effort to show the world that the US was not willing to continue a unilateral foreign policy, but rather was committed to maintaining the liberal order. The rise of China during this time was troubling for the United States as Washington realized that China was not a proponent of the liberal order. Obama tried to work with China, believing that cooperation with China would lead to a liberalization of China and would tie China in with the liberal order. However, China chose carefully in which areas to cooperate and was very wary about being tied to the liberal order. It didn't actively resist the liberal order, but it did keep the liberal order at a distance. Publicly, it did not denounce the liberal order, but privately Beijing worked toward the time that it could help usher in a new era of multipolarity. Obama realized that China was not only a global threat but also a significant regional threat to stability. Thus, he created a pivot to Asia in which the United States would focus on relations with many of the states in the region, trying to balance increasing Chinese influence. Thus, according to official policy, Washington stated that it wanted to increase the level of cooperation and alliance with New Delhi.

After the 2016 election in the United States, newly elected president Donald Trump began a new era of retrenchment and withdrawal from external alliances. He believed that the United States was not benefiting as much as it should have from those alliances. Specifically, Donald Trump believed that the European powers in NATO were not paying their share and were relying upon the United States to provide for their defense and their security. He believed that the problem with this was that the United States was forced to defend Europe while Europe was able to spend on their economies and expand their domestic economies to compete more effectively with the economy of the United States.

Trump believed very strongly that China was a great threat to the United States economically. Where Obama had tried to bring China into the global order, Trump believed that the only way to deal with China was to isolate it. Further, he believed that the United States and China were linked together too closely and that China was winning an economic war against the United States. Rather than attempt to ally the United States more with states that could stand up to China in the region, Trump attempted to raise tariffs on Chinese products and began a trade war with China. Instead of collaborating with India to balance against China's growing economic power in the region, Washington continued to pursue its goals unilaterally while discounting the role of its allies.

The COVID-19 crisis in 2020 exacerbated the difficulty of working with allies. Instead of working together to try to come up with a solution to the crisis, the Trump administration worked unilaterally to develop a vaccine and a strategy for dealing with the crisis. The Trump administration closed down borders and worked to continue to isolate the United States and to begin to extricate itself from a globalized world. That did not mean that relations between India and the United States became nonexistent, but the tenor of those relations changed. We now turn to a specific discussion of India's relations with the United States.

As discussed in the previous chapter, this volume aims to assess whether India will ally with status quo or revisionist states in its quest for great power status. Since attaining independence from the British Raj in 1947, India has remained nonaligned and has pursued diplomatic ties with all major powers including the United States and the Soviet Union. During the Cold War, India assumed a leadership role in the Non-Aligned Movement, adopting a "Third World" approach, which included maintaining diplomatic ties, trading relationships, and receiving aid from both First World and Second World states. In spite of its commitment to neutrality and nonalignment, over time India developed close ties with the Soviet Union, which resulted in long periods of alienation and altercation between India and the United States.

India and the United States share several values including strong support for democracy, the rule of law, free trade and markets, international institutions, and human rights. They also face common threats, such as a rising and increasingly aggressive China, terrorism, and religious extremism. They are also grappling with similar challenges such as the hazards of climate change and refugees from neighboring states. There are issues over which the two states disagree in principle and in practice. Some notable examples of the several topics of contention between the two states include agricultural subsidies and trade restrictions, American unilateralism and interference in the domestic affairs of other states, America's historic support for Pakistan including provision of weapons and technology, India's close ties with the Soviet Union/Russia, India's continued ties and trade with Iran in spite of US sanctions, and India's rejection of the Non-Proliferation Treaty and consequent decision to become a nuclear weapons state. We elaborate on several of these points of cooperation and contention below.

This chapter will examine Indo-US ties with an aim to assess the level of cooperation between India and the United States through the role of treaties and agreements as indicators of the strength of a bilateral relationship. Bilateral relations can be either ad hoc, meaning that the two states deal with issues as they arise, or they can be institutionalized, where the relationship is a cooperative one that has been carefully built to expand the relationship to mutually benefit both states. States that have institutionalized bilateral relations are much more likely to resolve disputes peacefully than those states that have an ad hoc relationship (Slobodchikoff 2013). To examine whether the cooperation between India and the United States is institutionalized or ad hoc, we explore the patterns of nested treaties between both countries to assess their levels of cooperation. Using methodology developed by Slobodchikoff (2013, 2014), we argue that higher levels of treaty nesting in the Indo-American bilateral treaty network would suggest that the two states are actively working to institutionalize their relationship.

However, we find little evidence of nesting in the treaty making patterns between the United States and India. Indo-US cooperation instead appears to be limited to specific issue areas. Much of their cooperation is taking place in the absence of formal agreements and can be characterized as ad hoc. This implies that while the United States is *currently* courting India as a capable and reliable ally to balance the rise of China in Asia, it has no intentions of forming a broad partnership with India that spills over into other issue areas. Based on the evidence examined, we do not expect the India-US strategic partnership to turn into a special relationship that the United States shares with close allies such as the United Kingdom, France, and Canada. The Indo-American relationship is driven solely by the rise of China's power and will fade if the threat dissipates (unlikely in the near future). We argue that this is a mistake on the part of the United States because it enables India to develop deeper cooperation with rivals such as Russia and China. In fact, in subsequent chapters we demonstrate that India has a deeper institutionalized bilateral relationship with Russia and China than it does with the United States. If the United States were to focus on building a cooperative relationship with India, it would be able to ensure that the challenge to the global order would be able to be contained. However, if it continues the way it currently has built its relationship with India, it may lose India when it comes time that China and Russia are powerful enough to directly challenge the United States for dominance of the global order.

We first examine the historical evolution of bilateral ties between India and the United States. We discuss the areas of cooperation as well as the areas of contention between the two countries. Next, we state our argument for why we expect treaty nesting to serve as an indicator of the strength of the bilateral relationship. We analyze the bilateral treaty network between India and the United States from 1947 to the present. Then, we present our findings that suggest that India and the United States have not institutionalized their relationship and continue to cooperate in an ad hoc manner, suggesting that the relationship is weak. Finally, we conclude with a discussion of the relevance of our findings for the future of Indo-American ties.

India-US Relations

In this section we give an overview of Indo-US relations.[1] During the Cold War, the Soviet Union became one of India's largest aid providers and trade partners as well as provider of military technology and weapons.[2] Thus, while officially maintaining its political neutrality, unofficially, India was considered to be in the Soviet sphere of influence. India and the Soviet Union also formed a treaty of friendship in 1971, signaling to the international community their close ties.[3]

Meanwhile, the United States became a close ally of India's neighbor and longtime rival, Pakistan. India and Pakistan have shared a troubled relationship ever since the partition of India by the British rulers resulted in the creation of the Islamic Republic of Pakistan in 1947. The two countries have fought three major wars and several militarized disputes between 1947 and the present. The United States served as an aid donor, weapons provider, and ally to Pakistan, thus leading to deteriorating ties between India and the United States.[4]

India tested the nuclear bomb and joined the elite group of nuclear states in 1998, further escalating tensions with the United States and much of the Western world. Relations improved between India and the United States only after the Bush administration removed economic sanctions and the two countries signed a nuclear agreement in 2005.

Since the second Bush administration lifted economic sanctions on India and entered into a nuclear treaty with it, relations between the United States and India have been largely positive. There is growing cooperation between the two countries in economic, political, and military domains. The strong Indian diaspora in North America continues to strengthen cultural and economic links between the two states. India was a key ally of the United States as the Obama administration sought to "pivot" or "rebalance" in Asia, given the rapid economic rise of China. The Trump administration also pursued

---

1. For detailed discussions of Indo-US relations, see Kronstadt (2005), Martin and Kronstadt (2007), Kapur and Ganguly (2007), Ganguly (2003), and Ganguly and Scobell (2005).

2. SIPRI Arms Transfer Dataset, https://www.sipri.org/databases/armstransfers

3. Treaty of Peace, Friendship and Cooperation between the Government of India and the Government of the Union of Soviet Socialist Republics, signed August 9, 1971.

4. SIPRI Arms Transfer Dataset, https://www.sipri.org/databases/armstransfers

similar goals in Asia—containing China and preserving freedom of navigation of the seas, and bolstering partnerships with regional powers such as Australia, India, and Japan. As China has become more and more assertive in Asia, regional powers like India have turned to external great powers like the United States for assistance in preventing China's domination of the region. As stated in the US National Security Strategy document released in May 2010, "The blossoming US-India friendship seems to be based on convergence of strategic interests and shared values of rules of law." The US and India share a strategic partnership based on their shared values as the world's two largest democracies as well as the connections among their people (White House 2010).

The 2017 US National Security Strategy states that "a geopolitical competition between free and repressive visions of world order is taking place in the Indo-Pacific region. The region, which stretches from the west coast of India to the western shores of the United States, represents the most populous and economically dynamic part of the world. The U.S. interest in a free and open Indo-Pacific extends back to the earliest days of our republic" (46). The 2017 US National Security Strategy welcomes "India's emergence as a leading global power and stronger strategic and defense partner" and it calls for more cooperation with the Quad—Japan, Australia, India, and the United States. It also pledges to "expand our defense and security cooperation with India, a Major Defense Partner of the United States, and support India's growing relationships throughout the region" (47). "The newly formulated strategy also welcomes India's rise as a 'leading global power' and emphasizes expanded defense ties with New Delhi. Notably, the framework appears focused on pulling India more intensively into regional activities" (Ayers 2018).

Chacko (2014) argues that power transitions bring about an "ontological" security concern for states due to changing identities and relationships. The United States is addressing such an ontological security concern resulting from the rise of China and the end of American unipolarity by establishing a special relationship with India. By establishing a close relationship with India, the United States is able to signal the universality of American ideas and institutions and enlist support for the current global order, which China is attempting to alter. Chacko (2014) further argues that while relations between India and the United States have improved, they continue to be hampered by the two countries' differing worldviews as well as self-perceptions.

It is worth emphasizing that while the diplomats from both countries pay lip service to the shared interests and values of both countries including their democratic regimes, as well as respect for human rights and the rule of law,

their friendship is based on common threats and joint security concerns ema-
nating from China. The two countries have started to cooperate on a much
larger scale in the last few years. This coincides with the rise of China as well
as its desire to reshape the global international order. Thus, balancing China's
power and influence in Asia remains the top catalyst for closer Indo-
American ties.

Data and Analysis

Methodology

We conduct a systematic analysis of all bilateral treaties between India and
the United States from 1947 to the present. India attained independence
from British rule in 1947 and began official diplomatic ties with the United
States. India and the US have signed a total of 54 bilateral treaties between
1947 and the present. The two states have created treaties on a wide range
of issues. Table 6 provides information on the total number of treaties created in each of the categories over the period of bilateral cooperation
between India and the United States.

India's Ministry of External Affairs (MEA) does not include agreements on defense and security in its database. India and the United States
have concluded several defense related agreements. While we discuss
these agreements and their impact on the relationship in subsequent sections of this chapter, we do not include them in the data compiled for
this chapter for reasons outlined below. It is also important to note that
most defense pacts are not efforts at building and institutionalizing relationships; rather, they are an ad hoc attempt at demonstrating military
power and conducting joint exercises between the military forces of the
states.

The MEA systematically excludes defense and security related agreements from its dataset. This includes agreements for military equipment and
technology procurements as well as decisions related to joint military exercises. The MEA includes all agreements that are signed at the level of foreign
minister and head of state and excludes agreements signed at the level of the
defense minister/secretary. While we have compiled information on some of
the landmark India–US defense and related agreements, we do not include
them in the data analysis to avoid introducing any bias into the data. Some of
the defense agreements may be missing from public records and to include
some while possibly missing others may skew our findings as well as our

understanding of the relationship. It is also possible that while agreements on some relationships such as that between India and the US are readily available, defense related information on other bilateral relationships such as those between India and China or India and Iran may be more difficult to come by. It is for this reason that we are relying on data made available by the MEA without alternations and additions.

More importantly, based on our coding methodology, any treaty that is explicitly referenced within an existing bilateral treaty is automatically introduced and included in our dataset (even if it is missing from the MEA's dataset). For example, when an India–US treaty explicitly references the United Nations Convention on Drugs and Trafficking, the multilateral convention is included in the dataset as other treaties are nested within it. We systematically apply this methodology to all treaties in all bilateral relationships in our study. Given the above, we find that not a single existing India–US treaty out of the 46 bilateral treaties included in the MEA's dataset makes any reference to any of the defense agreements that are not included in the dataset. None of the treaties in the dataset are nested within defense agreements. As such, we argue that while the defense agreements represent attempts at cooperation between the two states, they do not represent attempts to institutionalize the cooperation.

The cooperation score is the result of the total ties divided by the total number of treaties. Thus, if defense agreements were included in our analysis, the cooperation score would either be reduced or remain unchanged. At 0.5, the India-US cooperation score is firmly situated in the category of ad hoc cooperation and is in no danger of being affected by a small number of omitted agreements.

As suggested by the above data (table 6), there are only a small number of treaties in most of the issue categories noted above. These issue categories were provided by the government of India. As noted in table 6, the two states have created a very small number of bilateral treaties in most of the issue categories.[5] It is surprising that the two states have only formed a single treaty on issues that are a priority for both countries such as terrorism. There are either only a single treaty or a small number of bilateral treaties on most other issues including the environment, investment, illegal drug trafficking, and agricultural cooperation. This is a lost opportunity for both states, which seemingly have a lot of potential to cooperate on a wide range of issues. The only issue area on which there seems to be substantial and sustained coopera-

---

5. It is possible to group together some of the categories referenced in table 6. For instance, bilateral treaties in the areas of tax and investment can be reclassified as economic treaties.

Table 6. Indo-US Bilateral Treaties

Issue Area	Number of Treaties
Science/Technology	24
Cooperation	5
Diplomacy	2
Employment	1
Energy	5
Taxation	2
Health	1
Terrorism	1
Environmental	1
Economic	3
Agriculture Cooperation	1
Illegal Drug Trafficking	2
Education	1
Air Services	1
Investment	1

tion is science and technology. This broad category subsumes cooperation on space exploration, military technology, and other related issues.

Nesting and Lodestone Treaties

India's relationship with the United States is not at all institutionalized in the area of treaty formation. There are only a small number of treaties that seem central to the relationship. Below we discuss the lodestone treaties (see table 7) in the relationship.

The *Mutual Cooperation Agreement between India and United States of America for Reducing Demand, Preventing Illicit Use of Traffic in Drugs and for Matters Relating to Licit Trade in Opiates, Etc.* (INUSA15 in fig. 8) was signed in 1990. It is nested in the Convention on Narcotic Drugs and the Convention on Psychotropic Substances, both multilateral agreements. The *MOU between India and United States of America on Cooperative Measures to Increase Awareness of and Support for Efforts to Combat Production, Distribution and Use of Illegal Drugs* is nested within INUSA15 (fig. 8).

The *Joint Statement on Cooperation in Energy and Environment between India and United States of America* (INUSA23 in fig. 8) was signed in 2000 and is nested within multilateral agreements including the United Nations Framework Convention on Climate Change and Its Kyoto Protocol.

Table 7. Lodestone Treaties between India and the United States

Treaty Name	Year Signed	Degree Centrality	Issue Area
Mutual Cooperation Agreement between India and United States of America for Reducing Demand, Preventing Illicit Use of Traffic in Drugs and for Matters Relating to Licit Trade in Opiates, Etc	**1990**	3	Illegal Drug Trafficking
Joint Statement on Cooperation in Energy and Environment between India and United States of America	**2000**	3	Energy
Agreement on Science and Technology Cooperation between India and United States of America	**2005**	3	Science and Technology
MOU between the Department of Space and the Department of Science and Technology of the Government of the Republic of India and the National Aeronautics and Space Administration and the National Oceanic and Atmospheric Administration of the USA for Scientific Cooperation in the Areas of Earth and Atmospheric Sciences	**1997**	3	Science and Technology
Amended MOU	**2002**	3	Science and Technology
Agreement for Cooperation in Earth Sciences between India and United States of America	**2008**	2	Science and Technology
Framework Agreement between India and United States of America for Cooperation in the Exploration and Use of Outer Space for Peaceful Purposes	**2008**	3	Science and Technology

The *Agreement on Science and Technology Cooperation between India and United States of America* (INUSA28 in fig. 8) was signed in 2005 and is referenced by three subsequent bilateral treaties. These nested treaties include the *MOU on Agriculture Cooperation and Food Security between India and United States of America* and the *Agreement between India and United States of America on Cooperation on a Joint Clean Energy Research and Development Centre.*

We next discuss a group of four treaties that all serve as lodestone treaties in the relationship. The small cluster of treaties in the bottom left of the network map (fig. 8) all make reference to cooperation in the field of science and technology in general and cooperation in the areas of Earth and atmospheric sciences in particular. These four treaties are the following:

Fig. 8. Indo-US Treaty Network

- The *MOU between the Department of Space and the Department of Science and Technology of the Government of the Republic of India and the National Aeronautics and Space Administration and the National Oceanic and Atmospheric Administration of the USA for Scientific Cooperation in the Areas of Earth and Atmospheric Sciences* (listed as INUSA32 in fig. 8) was signed in 1997.
- The *Amended MOU between the Department of Space and the Department of Science and Technology of the Government of the Republic of India and the National Aeronautics and Space Administration and the National Oceanic and Atmospheric Administration of the USA for Scientific Cooperation in the Areas of Earth and Atmospheric Sciences* (listed as INUSA33 in fig. 8) was signed in 2002.
- The *Agreement for Cooperation in Earth Sciences between India and United States of America* (listed as INUSA31 in fig. 8) was signed in 2008.
- The *Framework Agreement between India and United States of America for Cooperation in the Exploration and Use of Outer Space for Peaceful Purposes* (listed as INUSA34 in fig. 8) was signed in 2008.

India and the United States first signed a memorandum of understanding (MOU) related to space exploration in 1997 and later amended it in 2002.

These MOUs included collaboration between the government of India's Departments of Space and Science and Technology and the US National Aeronautics and Space Administration (NASA) and National Oceanic and Atmospheric Sciences in the areas of Earth and atmospheric sciences. The two countries signed two related treaties in 2008, the *Agreement for Cooperation in Earth Sciences between India and United States of America* and the *Framework Agreement between India and United States of America for Cooperation in the Exploration and Use of Outer Space for Peaceful Purposes*. The latter is also nested within the international multilateral Convention on International Liability for Damage Caused by Space Objects.

None of the other treaties show any degree of nesting, indicating that they were ad hoc agreements dealing with important issues, but not attempts to institutionalize the relationship. As suggested by the network map (fig. 8), most of the treaties in the Indo-American dyad remain unlinked; the network map is composed of various disjointed sections. This suggests that Indo-American bilateral cooperation is taking place is an ad hoc manner. The states are not attempting to systematically link issues of cooperation to one another.

Issue linkage is a negotiation strategy that combines a number of issues and makes their outcome dependent on each other. It facilitates cooperation by increasing the bargaining range between states. States can make concessions on issues that are of low priority to them but of a higher priority to their negotiating partner, thus eliciting concessions on issues that may be of a higher priority to them compared to their negotiation partner (Davis 2004; Poast 2012). Research suggests that when states attempt to link seemingly nonrelated issues during negotiations or bargaining, then the issue linkage results in reducing the probability of treaty violation (Leeds and Savun 2007). However, in the Indo-American bilateral relationship, the two states are negotiating treaties in isolation; there is no spillover of cooperation from one issue area to another.

In addition to this, when several states attempt to strengthen cooperation by negotiating and signing a framework of cooperation, this often serves as a lynchpin or foundation to the relationship. Such a foundational agreement often results in becoming the lodestone treaty to the bilateral relationship. By linking all (or most) subsequent agreements to such a lodestone treaty, states are increasing the costs of violating individual treaties and hence reducing the probability of treaty violation, resulting in enhanced cooperation. We find that India and the United States lack such a foundational agreement. While they have negotiated treaties that serve as the basis for cooperation in specific issue areas (such as scientific and technological cooperation), there is no overarching agreement that is central to the relationship. The two states have termed their relationship a "Strategic Partnership" but this remains an informal term because they have not established a treaty of friendship or cooperation to formalize this concept (unlike other bilateral relationships such as the Indo–Russian relationship). In other words, their strategic partnership does not really exist yet.

Institutionalization

Based on the methodology developed by Slobodchikoff (2013) and discussed in chapter 2, institutionalization of cooperation within a dyad is measured as the outcomes of total ties (i.e., instances of nesting) divided by the total number of bilateral treaties between the two states. It is important to note that each treaty is an attempt at cooperation on a single issue. Tying treaties together begins to institutionalize the treaty within the overall relationship, thus building cooperation within the relationship. If total ties divided by the total number of treaties is less than 1, that means that the number of treaties is greater than the number of ties, meaning that there is only an attempt to cooperate on individual issue areas as opposed to building a cooperative relationship. Thus, the bilateral relationship is ad hoc. When total ties divided by the total number of treaties is greater than 1, it means that more effort was made at tying treaties to previous treaties, which institutionalizes cooperation within the relationship. Thus, a cooperation score of greater than 1 is indicative of institutionalized cooperation. Table 8 presents the level of institutionalization within the Indo-American dyad between 1947 and present. Throughout the course of bilateral cooperation, the cooperation score between India and the United States has been less than 0.5, suggesting that the dyad is in the phase of ad hoc cooperation. In 2017, the cooperation score for the Indo-American dyad increased to 0.5. This is interesting because it shows that both India and the United States have started to build their relationship, but still remain in an ad hoc state. Instead, they have reached a moderately cooperative relationship. If they continue to tie future treaties to prior treaties, they will eventually build an institutionalized cooperative relationship.

As depicted in the Indo-American network map (fig. 8), the two states have pockets of cooperation where treaties addressing specific issue areas are nested within each other as well as within larger multilateral agreements. However, treaty nesting is present to a limited extent; the bilateral treaty network is composed of smaller isolated networks where treaties on different issues are not linked to a foundational treaty of cooperation or to each other.

Table 8. Level of Institutionalization in the
Indo-American Dyad from 1947 to 2017

Year	Institutionalization Score
1947	0
1950	0.333
1960	0.50
1970	0.25
1980	0.187
1990	0.263
2000	0.357
2010	0.446
2017	0.50

Analysis

We study three different metrics of cooperation to determine the level of cooperation within the Indo-American dyad: (1) the total number of bilateral treaties between the two states; (2) the range of issues over which the two states cooperate; and (3) the institutionalization score within the dyad (calculated by the total number of ties/total number of bilateral treaties). We find that India and the United States have created a total of 54 bilateral treaties between 1947 and the present. This is much fewer than the number of treaties created between India and other states; for instance, India and Russia have signed over 200 bilateral treaties in the same time period whereas India and Japan have signed 80 bilateral treaties in the same time period.

Based on information provided in table 6, India and the United States appear to have formed treaties on a wide range of issues. However, there is only a single treaty or a very small number of treaties in all areas of cooperation, with the exception of science and technology. Much of the bilateral cooperation between the two countries is limited to one area—security related cooperation. There is limited cooperation in the economic and political spheres. This measure also suggests that cooperation between the two countries is limited to responding to common security threats and concerns. India and the United States have not made efforts to find additional areas of cooperation, in spite of the potential to do so.

Our third and final measure is related to the crux of this book: the role of nested treaties in serving to institutionalize cooperation between two states. By explicitly nesting new treaties within existing treaties, states enhance the probability of cooperation and reduce the probability of treaty violation. This is so because when a state violates a treaty that is nested within previous treaties, they are violating several treaties simultaneously. This is likely to result in increased costs and consequences of treaty violation as compared to violating a single, isolated treaty. As described above, we calculate the level of nestedness or institutionalization in a dyadic relationship using the total ties divided by the total treaties measure. When this measure is within the range of 0–1, it suggests *ad hoc* cooperation between the states, and when it is greater than 1, it suggests that the dyad exhibits *institutionalized* cooperation. The institutionalization score for the Indo-American dyad is 0.50, suggesting that it continues to be in the state of *ad hoc* cooperation.

Conclusion

This chapter begins by noting the many potential areas over which India and the United States have the ability to cooperate, producing mutually beneficial outcomes. These include cooperation in the dimensions of creating and supporting via resources a rules based international regime in the areas of counterterrorism, illegal trafficking (both of drugs and human beings), addressing climate change, maintaining liberal markets and a free trade economy, and supporting democratic regimes . . . to name just a few. While there has been some cooperation in many of the above-mentioned fields, the catalyst to speed up Indo-American cooperation has been the rise in China's power as well as its aggressive actions in Asia and beyond. India and China share a long territorial border that remains disputed; the two countries fought a war in 1962 that was decisively won by China. While the disputed border and associated territory remains a topic of contention, both sides are determined to address the dispute via diplomatic means. They continue to be trade partners and cooperate on a range of issues as well. Economic growth and development remains a top priority for both states and they are eager to avoid a militarized conflict that would severely damage their economies. The two countries are also nuclear powers, which undoubtedly serves as a deterrent against the escalation of low-level militarized disputes.

As described above, the United States has significantly enhanced its strategic and military cooperation with India in the last few years. India remains a vital component in US efforts to balance against the rise of China. India has the ability and the willingness to serve as a check on Chinese power and aggression in Asia. However, it is perplexing that, in spite of the many things that have the potential to bind India and the United States together, the two countries have invested very little in institutionalizing their cooperation. At present, Indo-American cooperation remains ad hoc, suggesting that ties between the two countries are weak. The United States has not made a sufficient effort to ensure that India is firmly within the American sphere of influence. As we demonstrate in subsequent chapters, India shares a warm and cooperation relationship with Russia. India and China also continue to cooperate over a range of issues, in spite of competing with each other for strategic dominance in Asia. By studying the Indo-American treaty networks we find that Indo-American ties are much weaker compared to India's other bilateral relationships.

Obama's pivot to Asia, and specifically the increased level of attention that Washington wanted to pay to New Delhi, did not fully materialize. If the US wants to develop a better relationship with India, it really has to begin to reach out, to cooperate in many other issue areas, and work to institutionalize the relationship. Otherwise, the relationship will continue to be ad hoc and not effective in balancing China's increasing power in the region.

While we end our analysis in 2017, the relationship between the United States and India has not significantly improved since then. If the United States wishes to improve its relationship with India, it must be willing to do so. Further, it must be willing to recognize that a relationship with Islamabad does not mean that it can't have a good relationship with New Delhi. In other words, it is possible for Washington to manage both relationships without putting either in jeopardy. While the relationship with Islamabad was incredibly important to maintain control in Afghanistan, the relationship with New Delhi is extremely important for the future of the global order.

5 • Indo-European Relations

Following World War II, the world was split into a bilateral hierarchical structure. On the one side was the Soviet Union and its allies, and on the other side was the United States and its allies. The Soviet Union and its allies promoted a communist ideology whereas the United States and its allies promoted the liberal order. This power structure continued until the end of the Cold War when the United States and its liberal order triumphed.

The United States relied upon many great powers to maintain its hegemony. Chief among those have been the Western European powers that had been allied with the United States during the Cold War. Specifically, France, Germany, and the United Kingdom have been the closest allies of the United States in Europe and globally. Each of these states has provided for the liberal order, and accepted and institutionalized that liberal order. Each of these states belongs to NATO, the collective security organization tasked with protecting the security of the member states adhering to the liberal order. Moreover, the European Union (EU) has further solidified the liberal order in Europe.

As France, Germany, the United Kingdom, and the EU are some of the greatest allies of the United States and the current liberal order, it is extremely important to examine their relationship with India. If India is a status quo power, then it should have cooperative relationships with these powers. However, if it has ad hoc relationships with these powers, this would be evidence to suggest that India is not a status quo power and might be rather a revisionist power.

In this chapter, we examine India's relations with these European states. While we recognize that the EU is not a state per se, we include the EU in our analysis to make sure that we have accounted for economic cooperation between India and the EU and its member states. The EU has authority to sign its own treaties with other states and is thus considered to be an important actor in international relations. It is important even though it does not have its own military. We will first examine India's relations with the EU as a whole and then we will examine India's relations with France, Germany, and the United Kingdom.

Indo-EU Relations

Prior to the end of the Cold War, India and the EU did not have much of a relationship. With the end of the Cold War, both India and the EU began intense cooperation. Much of the reason for this was that it was a chance to open new markets and increase trade. The collapse of the Soviet Union made it even more important that India develop new markets and new trade relationships.

As the EU became more and more institutionalized and became a supranational organization, cooperation increased between the two countries. However, the strategic partnership didn't fulfill its full potential (Wülbers 2010). The EU seemed to be more concerned with issues involving its member states than with truly creating a cooperative relationship with India.

The rise of China as a possible challenger to the global order created an impetus for the EU to further develop relations with India. The EU recognized that China's economic power was quickly overtaking that of most of the West and that the EU needed to balance China's economic power through new and deepening relationships with India (Goddeeris 2011; Jain and Pandey 2019). China's increased economic might made it imperative that the EU work closely with India especially in the second decade of the 21st century (Jain and Pandey 2019).

Even though the EU is an organization that has legal sovereignty and is able to sign treaties, most of those treaties focus on economics rather than security. The EU does not have its own security forces but leaves Europe's security to NATO and to the EU member states individually. Thus, it is not only important to analyze the relationship between India and the EU but also to look at the individual great powers in Europe and examine each of their relationships with India. We first discuss India's relations with the United Kingdom, and then turn to India's relations with France and Germany.

Indo-UK Relations

One of the United States' greatest allies in Europe is the United Kingdom. There is a long history of relationship between the United States and the

United Kingdom. While initially the United States fought the United Kingdom (then known as Great Britain) for independence, and again fought against the United Kingdom in 1812, the relationship nevertheless progressed. There was a shared history and language, and over time the relationship between the two states improved to the point that the United Kingdom was one of the United States' biggest supporters and best allies.

The United Kingdom has been wary of becoming too entangled in the European continent. Despite joining the EU, the United Kingdom was wary of becoming too reliant on Europe and did not appreciate the fact that the EU wasn't a supranational organization and some of the EU's decisions were a direct affront to British sovereignty. Instead, Britain forged closer ties with the United States and was one of the first states to support the United States after the terrorist attacks of September 11 and again when President George W. Bush decided to invade Iraq. While many states in Europe were not supportive of the invasion of Iraq, the United Kingdom was one of the stalwart supporters and helped the war effort by sending military troops to Iraq to aid the United States.

India and the United Kingdom have a long history. The United Kingdom colonized India and it wasn't until after World War II that India was able to gain its independence from the UK. Because of the historical ties, it is conceivable that India and the UK could have a long and positive cooperative relationship. However, the history of colonialization also could hamper the relationship between the two states. In this section, we examine the history of the relationship between the two states and then later in the chapter analyze whether or not they have a cooperative relationship or an ad hoc relationship.

As a former British colony, India shares much in common with the United Kingdom including shared ties and common values. The British influenced India's democratic polity and shaped India's political, economic, and social institutions. India's continued membership in the Commonwealth is considered a token of its close association with Britain (Banerji 1977).

Nevertheless, historical associations aside, an analysis of substantive criteria suggests that Indo-British ties are not as close as they would seem from examining the historical relationship. Today, India and the United Kingdom share a strategic partnership. Their joint membership in the Commonwealth has not translated into closer ties. Neither state has fully exploited the potential of the Commonwealth in realizing their domestic and foreign policy goals (Eliott 2017). In 1947, India's accession to the Commonwealth was lauded because of what it would mean for the organization itself; the Commonwealth would be able to act as a representative for smaller developing countries around the world that would not have a voice on the world stage otherwise and, in terms of population, India represented a majority of the Commonwealth's citizens. For the British, the Commonwealth provided an opportunity to continue to exert influence over and maintain close ties with their former colonies, thus leading to enhanced prominence on the global stage, which would be otherwise absent given their reduced economic and military power in the post–World War II period. While India remained a part of the Commonwealth even after becoming a republic in 1949, it never fully exploited the possibilities presented by the organization (Eliott 2017). The Commonwealth also saw a diminishment in its situation in the British political system when no preference was given to Commonwealth states in terms of development aid provided by the Foreign Office (Eliott 2017). Thus, while there was hope and scope for strong Indo-British ties in the aftermath of India's independence, due to various reasons it did not come to be.[1] The level of trade between India and the UK remains quite low—total bilateral trade in 2018–19 was valued at 9.3 billion.[2]

Indo-French and Indo-German Relations

India and France have a lot of mutual interests. First, both at times have advocated for a more multilateral approach to the world order. They have both been at times critical of the United States and its unilateral approach to decision-making. Moreover, both the French and the Indians are very interested in scientific cooperation especially in the areas of space exploration.

Both states have also cooperated in the area of defense. India is a very strong market for defense products, and the French have been very eager to deal with the Indians on this issue. Further, Indian and French scientists have cooperated in nuclear energy and other important defense-related industries. Trade between the two countries has increased tremendously over time. In fact, France and India consider themselves to be strategic partners.

Similar to its relationship with France, India and Germany both claim to

---

1. For a detailed discussion of Indo-British ties after 1947, see Banerji (1977) and *The Erosion of a Relationship: India and Britain since 1960* by Michael Lipton and John Firn (Oxford: Oxford University Press, 1975).

2. "India, UK Putting in Place Building Blocks for Trade Pact, Says UK High Commissioner," *Hindu Business Line*, January 30, 2020, https://www.thehindubusinessline.com/ne ws/world/india-uk-putting-in-place-building-blocks-for-trade-pact-says-uk-high-commissio ner/article30694644.ece

have a very good relationship with each other. German and Indian relations began in the early post–World War II era when India was one of the first states to recognize the Federal Republic of Germany. The leaders of both states, Konrad Adenauer of Germany and Jawaharlal Nehru of India, were both in very similar situations. Nehru needed to rebuild India after the long era of colonialization, and needed to focus on industrialization. Adenauer also needed to rebuild the Federal Republic of Germany following Germany's defeat in World War II. Both leaders found that they could work together rather easily to increase their cooperation (Rothermund 2010).

German companies have often found the Indian market to be lucrative and important. In 1994, DaimlerChrysler opened up a branch in India and called it Mercedes-Benz India. Since that time, German companies have cooperated with Indian engineers and Indian companies to expand their reach in India. While India operates in a trade deficit with Germany, their trade has increased tremendously through the 2000s (Khashimwo 2015). We now turn to an analysis of each relationship using network analysis.

Analysis of Indo-EU Relations

In terms of the relationship between India and the EU, there is some evidence of institutionalized cooperation. For example, as figure 9 shows, there are several issue areas that are addressed by the relationship. On the top right-hand side of figure 9 is a cluster of treaties that deal with space exploration (see fig. 9). The cluster of treaties on the left-hand side of figure 9 deal with technological innovation and trade. Because the EU mainly focuses on economic issue areas, it is not a surprise that such a big cluster is focused on technology and trade.

Although the first treaties between Europe and India were signed in 1971 (with the European Community, the predecessor of the EU), most of the treaties were signed after the Treaty of Rome in the early to mid-2000s. However, it is not until very recently that the relationship between India and the EU qualifies as a cooperative relationship. As table 9 shows, only starting in 2019 is the relationship cooperative with a measure of 1.08. Prior to that, there was cooperation but it was mainly ad hoc cooperation.

The two most central treaties determined by measuring treaty centrality are the joint declaration between India and the European Union on the Research and Innovation Center, which was signed in February 2012, and the cooperation agreement between India and the European Community on a partnership agreement that was focused on tariffs and trade. The partnership agreement on tariffs and trade was signed in 1993.

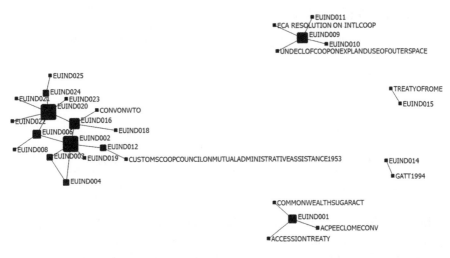

Fig. 9. Indo-EU Treaty Network

It is no surprise that most of the cooperation has to do with innovation and trade between India and the EU. The EU has mainly focused on facilitating trade among the member states of the EU, and has looked to expand European markets and trade overseas. What is a surprise, though, is that there have only been a total of 25 treaties signed between the two entities. Further, while some cooperation took place prior to the beginning of the 21st century, over 70 percent of the treaties signed between the EU and India were signed in 2000 and beyond. In other words, India and the EU have really begun to cooperate more fully after 2000, which was when China began its tremendous economic growth.

Table 9 also shows that only 25 treaties have been signed between the EU and India. This should not be a surprise, as Indo-European cooperation takes place not only with the EU but also with other EU member states. Specifically, Indo-European cooperation takes place between India and the other great powers in Europe. We now turn to analyzing the relationship between India and the UK.

Analysis of Indo-UK Relations

The relationship between India and the United Kingdom is a problematic one in that it carries a lot of baggage of colonialism. On the one hand, it would make sense to have a cooperative institutionalized relationship

Table 9. India-EU Cooperation

Year	Treaties	Ties	Cooperation Score
1950	—	—	0
1960	—	—	0
1970	—	—	0
1980	4	3	.75
1990	5	4	.8
2000	8	6	.75
2010	23	20	.87
2019	**25**	**27**	**1.08**

between the two states because of their shared history and shared institutions. On the other hand, the United Kingdom was a colonizer and ruled India tightly, leading to resentment toward the United Kingdom by India.

Figure 10 illustrates the relationship between the two states by showing a treaty map. It is evident by looking at this treaty map that the relationship between the two states is very ad hoc and not institutionalized. There are many different smaller areas of cooperation, but no large-scale cooperation or attempts at joining together and institutionalizing cooperation (see fig. 10). One of the most central treaties to that relationship can be seen on the left-hand side of figure 10. This is the Declaration between India and the UK on Cooperation in Providing a Safer World. This declaration has to do with terrorism and cooperation to combat terrorism.

A deeper exploration of the relationship between the two states shows that the initial impressions given by the treaty map are accurate (see table 10). As table 10 shows, at no point in the relationship does it become cooperative. Instead, the relationship has always been ad hoc, and by 2019 it only rates a .53 cooperation score. This is a little bit surprising as one would expect a fair amount of cooperation between the two states. However, it is evident that both states deal with issues as they come up rather than looking at a relationship as being of strategic interest to both states, which would warrant institutionalizing the relationship.

We find only seven instances in which a bilateral Indo-British treaty is nested within other bilateral Indo-British bilateral treaties during the entire period of study from 1947 to 2018. Also, we find 11 instances where a bilateral Indo-British treaty is nested within a multilateral convention including the Convention on International Aviation, the United Nations Commission on International Law, United Nations Security Council Resolution 1373, the Brahimi Report, the Bonn Agreement, the Kyoto Protocol, the United

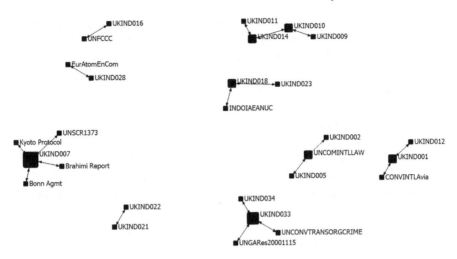

Fig. 10. Indo-UK Treaty Network

Nations Framework Convention on Climate Change, the Agreement between the Government of India and the IAEA for the Application of Safeguards to Civilian Nuclear Facilities, the Statement of Civil Nuclear Cooperation with India, the Treaty Establishing the European Atomic Energy Community, UN General Assembly Resolution of November 15, 2000, and the UN Convention on Transnational Organized Crime.

None of the other treaties show any degree of nesting, indicating that they were ad hoc agreements dealing with important issues, but not attempts to institutionalize the relationship. As suggested by the network map (fig. 9), most of the treaties in the Indo-American dyad remain unlinked; the network map is composed of various disjointed sections. This suggests that the Indo-American bilateral cooperation is taking place in an ad hoc manner. States are not attempting to systematically link issues of cooperation to one another. Given the low number of nested treaties, the cooperation score between India and the United Kingdom reaches a high of .61 and is at .52 in 2018. Based on the methodology described earlier, a cooperation score less than 1 suggests ad hoc cooperation between the two states.

Lodestone Treaties

The two lodestone treaties in this relationship are the New Delhi Declaration India and United Kingdom Partnership for Better and Safer World (listed as UKIND007 in fig. 9) and the MOU between India and the

United Kingdom of Great Britain and Northern Ireland Regarding Co-Operation and the Exchange of Information for the Purposes of Combating International Criminality and Tackling Serious Organised Crime (listed as UKIND033 in fig. 9).

The New Delhi Declaration India and United Kingdom Partnership for Better and Safer World (listed as UKIND007 in fig. 9) was signed in 2002 and is nested within the following multilateral agreements: the United Nations Security Council (UNSC) Resolution 1373,[3] the Brahimi Report,[4] the Bonn Agreement,[5] and the Kyoto Protocol.[6] The Delhi Declaration was signed between Prime Ministers Atal Bihari Vajpayee and Tony Blair to reaffirm the Indo-British partnership and find new areas of cooperation between the two countries. Signed in the aftermath of the 9/11 terrorist attacks in America, the declaration condemns the attack and pledges the two states to cooperate on counterterrorism measures, also invoking UN Security Council Resolution 1373. It noted cooperation on setting up a sovereign regime in Afghanistan, invoking the Bonn Agreement for establishing a democratic government in Afghanistan. Other topics of cooperation noted in the declaration include eliminating poverty, HIV/AIDS, sustainable development, education, and science and technology; the UK agreed to enhance its overall aid to India to tackle these issues. The agreement noted that bilateral trade between the two countries had reached five million pounds in 2001, with UK being India's largest trading partner in Europe and the second largest in the world. In addition to noting the rising trend of bilateral investments in each other's economies, the two countries pledged to enhance economic cooperation to strengthen their friendship.

The *MOU between India and the United Kingdom of Great Britain and Northern Ireland Regarding Co-Operation and the Exchange of Information for the Purposes of Combating International Criminality and Tackling Serious Organised Crime* (listed as UKIND033 in fig. 9) was signed in 2018 and is nested within the Agreement between the Government of India and the Government of the United Kingdom and Northern Ireland concerning the Investigation of the Proceeds and Instruments of Crime (34 in fig. 9), the United Nations Convention on Transnational Organized Crime, and the UN General Assembly Resolution of November 15, 2000. This

---

3. https://www.unodc.org/pdf/crime/terrorism/res_1373_english.pdf

4. Report of the Panel on the United Nations Peacekeeping, Aug 17, 2000.

5. Agreement on Provisional Arrangements in Afghanistan Pending the Re-establishment of Permanent Government Institutions (Bonn Agreement), May 12, 2001, United Nations Treaty Database.

6. http://kyotoprotocol.com/

Table 10. India-UK Cooperation

Year	Treaties	Ties	Cooperation Score
1950	—	—	0
1960	2	1	.5
1970	3	1	.33
1980	3	1	.33
1990	3	1	.33
2000	8	2	.25
2010	21	13	.62
2019	36	19	.53

MOU deals with establishing a framework that helps to exchange information such as criminal records, immigration records, and intelligence to aid in combatting transnational crime. As demonstrated by the treaty network map (fig. 9), both lodestone treaties are connected to each other. This suggests that combatting international terrorism and organized crime is crucial to both countries.

Similar to the relationship between India and the EU, India and the UK really had very few attempts at cooperation until the early 2000s. After that, they began to cooperate more. In fact, prior to 2000, only eight treaties had been signed. This is a very small number, but seems very similar to the EU. Although most of the treaties were signed after 2000, only 36 treaties were signed. This is more than the number signed by the EU and India, but there was less overall cooperation.

The Indo-British bilateral treaty network suggests that the relationship is rife with missed opportunities by both states. While there is much talk of a strategic partnership and a "special relationship" between India and the United Kingdom, few concrete steps have been taken by either country to cement ties and institutionalize the relationship. In the absence of deeply institutionalized ties, the interactions between the two countries remain ad hoc; they sometimes achieve cooperation on issues that are significant to both states, and more often miss the mark. For instance, India and the UK have been discussing a free trade agreement for a long time; it may finally become a reality in the post–BREXIT scenario, but it has been a long time in the making. Also, the United Kingdom has failed to capitalize on India's domestic market in the same way as China and other countries, in spite of having a head start in this area. The United Kingdom has also failed to penetrate India's defense market in spite of having historical ties to the country. The Commonwealth has failed to achieve the desired results in terms of binding together the former colonies to the UK. While a member of the

Commonwealth, as well as a robust participant in the activities of the Commonwealth, India does not collaborate with the United Kingdom on its foreign policy; the goals of the two countries do not necessarily align in several issue areas. The United Kingdom simply does not have the means to exercise control over its formal colonies such as India.

The fact that the UK has not invested time and effort into creating nested bilateral treaties with India has resulted in the lack of deeply institutionalized ties with its former colony. Meanwhile, countries such as France have capitalized on the opportunity by forming a cooperative relationship with India. It is puzzling that we find deeply institutionalized ties between India and France and not between India and the United Kingdom. It is further puzzling that France has formed an extensive bilateral treaty network with India and the two countries are cooperating over sectors such as railways and space technology. Given its historical ties to India, as well as its advanced knowledge of the Indian railway system, the United Kingdom can be presumed to have a leading position in developing and updating India's vast system of railways. A large proportion of this heavily populated country is dependent on India's sprawling and expanding system of rail transportation. Yet the United Kingdom has failed to capitalize on this opportunity.

The implications of this are severe for the United Kingdom. By failing to invest time, effort, and resources in maintaining close cooperation with one of its largest and most lucrative former colonies, the United Kingdom lost the opportunity to maintain influence over India and its foreign policy direction. Today, the United Kingdom is attempting to woo India given its economic potential and the size of its domestic market, as well as its rising stature in the international arena. In an attempt to revive and reenergize their current relationship, the United Kingdom is once again attempting to invoke historical ties with India. However, it will be an uphill battle for the UK given that there are few substantive areas with a strong base for cooperation between the two countries.

Analysis of Indo-French Relations

Contrary to the two cases that we have analyzed so far in this chapter, there seems to be much more cooperation between India and France than there has between either India and the UK or India and the EU (see fig. 11). As figure 11 shows, there are many fewer isolated nodes of cooperation, and much more evidence of tying together the treaties through nesting. In other words, there seems to be a much more deliberate attempt at institutionalizing cooperation than there was in the other two cases we have examined so far.

In figure 11 the size of the treaty node is set to degree of centrality. There are two very obvious central treaties and both are in the top cluster of figure 11: INFRA055 and INFRA031. INFRA031 deals with safeguards and management of nuclear energy, while INFRA055 deals with space and space exploration. Even though both of these are distinct categories, they are both linked to each other. Each of these central treaties were also nested within major multilateral treaties. The multilateral treaties are listed by treaty name rather than by treaty number. So it is very easy to see how the two types of treaties are interconnected by looking at figure 11. For example, the Convention on the International Liability and Damages of Space Objects is a major multilateral treaty that is tied to INFRA055.

Despite the fact that figure 11 shows a much more institutionalized form of cooperation between India and France than there has been between either India and the EU and India and the UK, when we look at table 11 we can see that it isn't until 2019 that India and France achieved an institutionalized cooperative relationship. In this way, the relationship between the two states unfolds in similar fashion to the other two that we have analyzed so far in this chapter (see table 11). In fact, it is only after 2010 that there really is an intense attempt to institutionalize cooperation. By 2010, the cooperation score between the two states was only .55, whereas the cooperation score jumped to 1.18 in 2019. The score of 1.18 between France and India is higher than the cooperation score of 1.08 between India and the EU. Further, as table 11 shows, almost half of the treaties between India and France were signed during the decade following 2010. That is a tremendous number of treaties, and it indicates the attempts by both states to institutionalize their relationship because they really worked to link the new treaties to previous treaties in the relationship as well as to other multilateral treaties.

In total, India and France signed 80 treaties. This is more than the number of treaties signed between India and the EU and India and the UK combined. Sixty-one treaties have been signed by both India and the EU and India and the UK, whereas India and France have signed 80 treaties. The number of treaties signed in addition to the number of ties and the level of institutionalization of cooperation clearly shows the importance of France to India and vice versa. The question, however, is whether the cooperation is limited to issue areas in which both states have a vested interest, such as space travel and nuclear energy, or if they have truly begun to develop a strategic cooperative relationship. It may be too early to parse this out, as much of the institutionalization has occurred in the last decade. However, the institu-

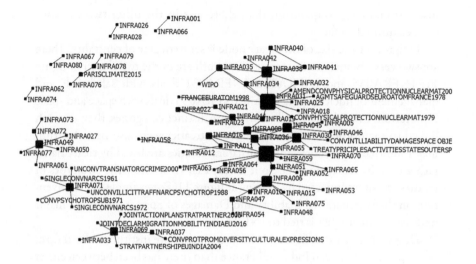

Fig. 11. Indo-France Treaty Network

Table 11. India-France Cooperation

Year	Treaties	Ties	Cooperation Score
1950	1	1	1
1960	4	1	.25
1970	7	1	.14
1980	11	3	.27
1990	16	7	.44
2000	21	8	.38
2010	42	23	.55
2019	**80**	**94**	**1.18**

tionalization has overlapped with the era in which Chinese power has grown tremendously and China has become a threat to other states in its region. In other words, it is natural to question whether India is cooperating with France to balance the power of China, which has been suggested by some of the other scholars who have studied this relationship, or whether the two states are really developing an institutionalized cooperation for their own benefit. It is also possible that the answer to this question is some combination of the two.

Whichever the case, India and France have developed an institutionalized cooperative relationship that looks like it will continue into the future. As energy needs increase and states move away from fossil fuels, nuclear

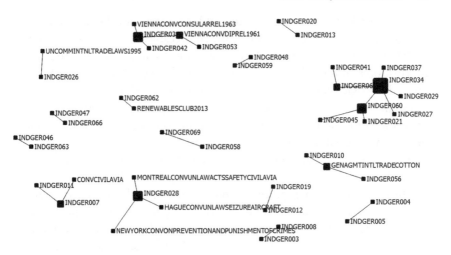

Fig. 12. Indo-Germany Treaty Network

energy will become even more important. Similarly, space exploration and resources from space such as iron from asteroids and other celestial materials may become more important in the future. Thus, it looks as though India and France will continue to cooperate and to institutionalize their cooperation even further. We now turn to an examination of India's relationship with Germany.

Analysis of Indo-German Relations

Despite the fact that India and Germany have quite a few areas where they could cooperate, figure 12 shows that they really have ad hoc cooperation (see fig. 12). Several different nodes of treaties are tied together, but there is no overarching structure to indicate institutionalization of the cooperative relationship. Although there is some treaty nesting, it is clear that the relationship is not an institutionalized cooperative relationship.

One of the most central treaties of the relationship is seen on the right-hand side of figure 12 and is labeled INDGER 034. This is not even technically a treaty, but an MOU on the establishment of an Indo-German technology center. This is related to industries such as the automobile industry. It should be noted that the fact that India and Germany have an MOU as the most central node in their cooperative relationship it is extremely important. The most central node in a relationship should normally be a treaty since a treaty is a legal agreement and is enforceable in international courts of arbitration. An MOU, however, is not legally enforceable. That is not to say that MOUs are not important. MOUs allow leaders and negotiators to state information that is not legally binding, thus making the MOUs more accurate and less rigid than treaties and official agreements. Thus, MOUs serve an important function. They indicate the desires and thoughts behind specific actions and often lay the groundwork for future cooperation. In fact, MOUs often are negotiated as vigorously as treaties and agreements, with the biggest difference being the legal binding of a specific treaty or agreement that the MOU does not possess.

There are several other agreements that are also central to the relationship but do not possess the amount of degree centrality that the MOU possesses. Of all of the four cases discussed in this chapter, the Indo–German relationship is the only one to have an MOU with the highest measure of degree centrality. Table 12 shows the cooperation scores for this relationship. It is important to note that there have only been 39 treaties signed between India and Germany. That's more than were signed by India and the EU or India and the UK. However, it is still much less than the number of treaties signed by India and France.

Table 12 also shows that the relationship between India and Germany never reaches the level required for institutionalized cooperation. In fact, the cooperation score never even reaches .5. This means that India and Germany really did not work on institutionalizing their relationship but focused on specific issues of cooperation rather than building a cooperative relationship. While Germany and India signed more treaties than either India and the EU or India and the UK, the relationship between India and Germany still had the lowest measure of cooperation (see table 13).

Table 13 shows all the cooperation scores of the European powers with India over time. Only two of the relationships have achieved cooperative relationships: India and the EU and India and France. The relationships between India and the UK and between India and Germany failed to reach the status of being an institutionalized cooperative relationship. Further, the table shows that while the relationships between India and the EU and India and France are institutionalized cooperative relationships, they only reached the status of an institutionalized cooperative relationship by 2019. Prior to that, all of the relationships were considered to be ad hoc. It seems that by 2019 an inflection point had been reached and that there was more of an attempt to create a strategic relationship between India and the European continent. However, the data are too recent to be able to make a strong determination as to either the future of the relationship or the strength of a strategic alliance.

Table 12. India-Germany Cooperation

Year	Treaties	Ties	Cooperation Score
1950	1	0	0
1960	6	1	.17
1970	12	5	.42
1980	25	7	.28
1990	25	7	.28
2000	27	8	.30
2010	39	16	.41
2019	39	16	.41

Table 13. Cooperation Scores for India's Relationship with European Powers

Year	EU	UK	France	Germany
1950	0	0	1	0
1960	0	.5	.25	.17
1970	0	.33	.14	.42
1980	.75	.33	.27	.28
1990	.80	.33	.44	.28
2000	.75	.25	.38	.30
2010	.87	.62	.55	.41
2019	**1.08**	.53	**1.18**	.41

If India is to be a status quo power, it really needs to have developed cooperative relationships and specifically institutionalized cooperative relationships with the great powers in Europe. The reason for this is because the European great powers are the biggest and most ardent allies of the United States and the liberal order. In the international order, the most powerful state and the global hegemon is the United States. Right below the United States in the hierarchy of the international order are the European great powers. Thus, it is extremely important to determine India's relationship with these European states, which provides an important context for understanding India's place within the global order. Is India a status quo power or is it a revisionist power? It is much too early in the analysis of this book to make a final determination as to India's position within the global order. However, since India does not have an institutionalized cooperative relationship with the United States, and it does not have long-standing institutionalized relationships with most of the European powers, it is natural to be skeptical of the idea that India is a status quo power. The fact that there is an institutionalized level of cooperation with both the EU and France indicates that there is a possibility that India could indeed become a status quo power. It currently is not. Instead, more analysis needs to be done to compare India's relationship with the status quo powers to India's relationship with the revisionist powers. In the next chapter, we will analyze India's relationship with Japan, which is the main ally of the United States in the Pacific region and a great power in its own right. It is a regional power, and if there exists evidence that India is trying to ally itself with the status quo powers to balance China's power in the region, then we should be able to see evidence of an institutionalized cooperative relationship between Japan and India.

6 • Indo-Japanese Relations

In 1945, the United States used two large atomic weapons to end World War II. The atomic bombs that landed on Hiroshima and Nagasaki in Japan not only ended World War II, but drastically ushered in an atomic era. So many people died in the blasts that warfare and the use of atomic weapons would drastically change the world order.

Japan surrendered to the United States and as part of that agreement agreed never to adopt an army or nuclear weapons. The United States in return offered to maintain the peace and to protect the sovereignty of Japan by protecting its security. In other words, while ensuring that the United States would not have to face a resurgent Japan in the future, the United States constrained itself from withdrawing from East Asia.

The United States invested heavily in the economy of Japan after the war. While initially the Japanese economy had to be rebuilt from scratch, very soon Japan became an economic powerhouse especially with new technology and the automobile industry. Japan led much of the world in science and technology and robotics. It could invest its revenues into the economy and into building up its infrastructure rather than supporting the defense industry, which was upheld by the United States.

The United States maintained its military presence in Japan and, following the Korean War, also maintained a significant presence in South Korea. The presence of US forces in East Asia assured that the US was heavily invested in the region and would prevent a challenge to the global order from emerging there. Specifically, the US military was concerned with isolating both China and the Soviet Union.

The end of the Cold War meant that the US did not need such a heavy military presence in East Asia. However, North Korea began pursuing nuclear weapons and was constantly a threat to South Korea. Thus, while the US did withdraw some forces, nevertheless it maintained an active presence in the region.

Japan is a central piece of the United States' strategy to maintain the global order in East Asia. While Japan is not a traditional great power, nevertheless it is a strong ally of the United States, a regional economic powerhouse, and an important piece to maintaining the US's position of primacy in the world. Thus, if India were to be a status quo power, it would need to develop a cooperative relationship with Japan and work with Japan to limit China's growth and power. We now turn to an examination of the relationship between India and Japan to see how cooperative their relationship is.

History of Indo-Japanese Ties

While literature on the early history of the relationship between the India and Japan is scarce, Aripta Mathur's book *India-Japan Relations: Drivers, Trends and Prospects* is likely the best effort at detailing the historical relationship. Mathur (2012) explains that Japan and India first established contact during the sixth century and that the spread of Buddhism was the common link that led to this meeting. As a common cultural characteristic, this allowed the relationship between the states to grow and expand and in the eighth century the first Indian Buddhist bishop was permanently placed in Japan (Mathur 2012). Religion would remain the main point of contact between the two states for the next millennia.

By the late 19th century, growing animosity between Western colonial governments and their Asian subjects would further bind the two states together. Throughout Asia, only Japan, Thailand, and Nepal escaped colonial rule by Western powers. This resulted in growing unrest in the region, culminating in the development of Pan-Asianism or the idea of Asian nationalism (Mathur 2012). Pan-Asianism developed in Japan in the latter part of the 19th century as a counter to Western hegemony. Due to colonization by Western powers, Japan became convinced that the only way to preserve Asian cultures and nations was to present a united front against Western encroachment. Stolte and Fischer-Tiné (2012, 70) state that "Japan became the forerunner of an alternative Asian modernity." During this period, Indians created youth organizations in Japan where Asian nationalism was espoused. Indians attempted to gain the support of Japan in its quest for independence and the idea of an "Asian association of states" under the leadership of Japan was first put forth and many members of the Indian National Congress began to call for a unified India, China, and Japan (Stolte and Fischer-Tiné 2012, 12). Upset by the influence the Japanese were having on

Indian youth, the British banned Indian students from visiting Japan without British consent.

Relations between India and Japan remained solid even as Japan became a colonial power in its own right and Indian nationalism began to grow in the shadow of Japanese pan-Asianism. India so looked to Japan as a role model of nationalism that when the *swadeshi* movement, the precursor of Modi's "Make in India" campaign, aimed at freeing India from foreign goods, was implemented in 1905, Japanese goods were exempted (India Today 2015). Mathur (2012, 6) states that "a prominent Indian newspaper *Kesari* clearly called on people to choose Japanese goods over all other foreign manufactured ones." The Japanese victory over Russia in the Russo-Japanese War was seen as a model of how Asian states should deal with European colonizers (Mathur 2012). "Indian leaders like Gandhi, Nehru, Gopal Krishna Gokhale and Bal Gangadhar Tilak were all unanimous in their jubilation over Japanese victory" (Mathur 2012, 5). While the 1910 occupation of Korea, the 21 demands made to China at the end of World War I, and later the attack on Manchuria did put strains on the relationship due to Japan's increasing imperialism, trade and diplomacy between the two nations never halted (Stolte and Fischer-Tiné 2012). During this time frame, trade between the two nations was high due to the Japanese spinning industries' need for cotton and India's ability to produce the commodity. This was disrupted briefly by the Sino-Japanese War and, in 1934, a trade war between the two states erupted due to Japanese import restrictions (Farley 1939). Regardless of the tensions, the two states remained relatively close throughout World War II even as Japan attacked India in the Battle of Kohima and Imphal in which Indian nationalists and Japanese troops were defeated by British and Royal Indian forces (Mathur 2012). The ties between India and Japan were most lavishly expressed in 1946 during the International Military Tribunals for the Far East when Indian judge Radha Binod Pal became the only one of 11 Allied justices to find Japan's military leaders not guilty of war crimes (Onishi 2007). The significance of this to the Japanese people cannot be underestimated as a monument was erected in Japan to the judge in 2005. Additionally, in 2007, Prime Minister Shinzo Abe addressed the Indian congress stating that "Justice Pal is highly respected even today by many Japanese for the noble spirit of courage he exhibited during the International Military Tribunal for the Far East" (Onishi 2007, 4).

During the Cold War, Japan and India's relationship was tense at times as India tilted toward the Soviet Union and Japan toward the United States. Additionally, Japan was upset with Indian proliferation and nuclear tests in

1974 due to its natural antinuclear status (Mathur 2012). However, not all was dark for the two states during this time. Japanese money and technology began to pour into India in the 1980s as Suzuki Motor Company partnered with Indian carmaker Maruti to form Maruti Suzuki India, which built plants and manufactured the Maruti 800 (Ministry of Foreign Affairs Japan 2018). The car became known as the car that changed India due to the fact that it was affordable, reliable, and for the first time Indians could travel long distances quickly and efficiently (Kalavalapalli, Raj, and Shah 2014). This was one bright point in an otherwise lackluster period in Indian-Japanese relations. Following the Cold War, the 1990s were actually worse with Japan cutting off all aid to India in 1998 due to Indian nuclear tests and demanding that India join the Comprehensive Test Ban Treaty (Chengappa 2000). Regardless, the 21st century would usher in a new age in Indo-Japanese relations as Chinese hegemony in the region began to become a greater threat.

Modern Indo-Japanese Relations

Beginning in 2000, coinciding with the rapid rise to power in China, a new relationship between India and Japan blossomed as Japanese prime minister Yoshiro Mori visited India where the Japan-India Global Partnership was signed. This was an all-inclusive economic and security partnership that aimed to encourage security, stability, and prosperity in Asia. For the first time Japan used the term "Global Partnership" in relation to any state other than the United States (Ghosh 2008). One important event in 2000 that marked growing military cooperation between India and Japan was the visit of Indian defense minister George Fernandes, the first visit by an Indian defense minister to Japan in the nation's history (Ghosh 2008). This showed a new military component to Indian-Japanese relations. That same year, the Indian and Japanese coast guards conducted joint exercises and command exchanges and, in 2002, India and the United States began the annual Malabar naval exercises, where Japan has become a regular participant (Lynch 2017). In 2006 and 2007, the global partnership was expanded to further encompass defense and cover new areas such as nuclear energy and was upgraded to strategic partnership (Ghosh 2008). It was during this time that the two nations decided to hold annual defense meetings. While naval exercises have become routine over the past two decades, in 2018, India and Japan launched joint land exercises for the first time, ushering in a new era of Indo-Japanese military relations. Indian colonel Aman Anand stated that the exercises were "yet another step in deepening strategic ties including closer defense cooperation between the two countries" (Panda 2018, 6). More recently, India and Japan have decided to hold a two plus two dialogue between their defense and foreign ministers. The growing special relationship between India and Japan is being driven by a number of factors including the desire to build an Asian strategic framework that can balance the rise of China (Basu 2014; Brewster 2010; Mukherjee 2018; Narayanan 2016; Panda 2012, 2014; Paul 2012; Yoshimatsu 2019; Rajago-palan 2020). The creation of strategic partnerships and security coopera-tion shows that India and Japan are balancing against China as China con-tinues to grow as a hegemonic force in the region (Chadha 2020). This becomes further evident through a comprehensive look at the treaties that have been signed by India and Japan since the end of World War II.

Despite the strategic importance of balancing Chinese regional power, India and Japan have nevertheless formed a special relationship that is not only designed to balance Chinese power but is an important strategic alli-ance that benefits both states regionally and economically (Baruah 2016). While President Obama promised a pivot to Asia, the Trump administration reached out to improve relations with North Korea, started a trade war with China, and began withdrawing from its alliance with Japan. Thus, the rela-tionship between India and Japan is even more important if they seek to bal-ance the power of China. They can no longer rely only on the United States, but must work together to ensure regional security.

We now turn to an analysis of the relationship between India and Japan to determine if their cooperation is institutionalized or ad hoc. We conduct a systematic analysis of all bilateral treaties between India and Japan between 1947 and 2018. The two countries have signed a total of 79 bilateral treaties during this time period.[1] To provide some context, India has signed 168 bilateral treaties with its close ally Russia, 163 treaties with China, and 58 with the United States in the same period. Thus, the total number of treaties between India and Japan is not an anomaly in either direction. We limit our analysis to all bilateral treaties signed between India and Japan. Multilateral treaties are included in the network map (fig. 13)[2] only when they are explic-itly referenced by a bilateral agreement, that is, when a bilateral treaty is nested within it.

Table 14 provides a comparison of the levels of cooperation based on

---

1. The first bilateral treaty between India and Japan was not signed until 1952, the Treaty of Peace Between India and Japan.

2. The node sizes in figure 13 are set according to degree centrality. Thus, the larger the treaty node, the more central the treaty is to the bilateral relationship. These treaties are the lodestone treaties of the relationship.

Table 14. Indo-Japanese Cooperation Issue Areas

Issue Category	Number of Treaties
Agricultural Cooperation	2
Aid	1
Air Services	1
Biodiversity	1
Cooperation	14
Commerce	2
Climate Change	1
Communication	2
Culture	2
Economic and Technical Assistance	7
Education	4
Energy	10
Investment	1
Health Care Cooperation	3
Law	1
Olympic Cooperation	1
Railways	1
Security Cooperation	1
Science and Technology	8
Social Security	1
Space Cooperation	2
Tourism	1
Taxation	5
Trade	2
World War II Ending	1

treaties between India and Japan. As in any bilateral relationship, the Indo-Japanese relationship starts with a score of 0, which suggests the absence of any cooperation. However, over the next few decades, the total ties/total treaties score quickly jumps, finally crossing the threshold of 1 in 2018. As explained above, states with a ties/treaty score of less than 1 are considered to demonstrate ad hoc cooperation and states with a ties/treaty score greater than 1 are considered to demonstrate institutionalized cooperation. Interestingly, India and Japan have entered a phase of institutionalized cooperation.

Indo-Japan Treaty Network

Figure 13 provides a network map of all Indo-Japanese treaties. Each treaty is represented as a node on the network map. When one treaty is nested

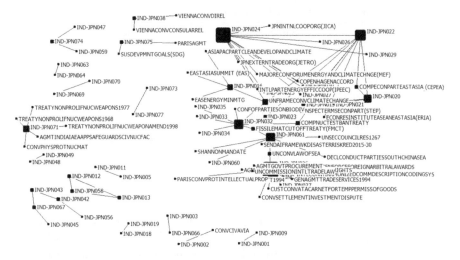

Fig. 13. Indo-Japan Treaty Network

within another treaty, the connection between the two treaties is represented by an arrow linking the two treaties. The higher the number of treaties nested within a treaty, the larger the size of the node representing that treaty. As depicted in the network map, there is a high density of nesting within the Indo-Japanese treaty network. There are also several large nodes; these are the lodestone nodes that are most significant to the relationship. Table 14 provides information on the category of issues over which the two states have negotiated agreements. Table 15 provides information on the cooperation score (the total number of ties/total number of treaties) for the Indo-Japanese dyad. Table 15 also provides information on the number of bilateral treaties formed in each decade.

Lodestone Treaties

Below we discuss the lodestone treaties in the relationship. The lodestone treaties are calculated using the degree centrality measure. Each lodestone treaty is also prominently depicted in the network map presented in figure 13.

Comprehensive Economic Partnership Agreement between India and Japan (Treaty Number INDJPN36 in fig. 13): This treaty signed by the two countries in 2011 seeks to "promote trade and investment through the establishment of clear and mutually advantageous rules as well as regulatory coopera-

Table 15. Indo-Japanese Cooperation Score

Year	Cooperation Score	Number of Treaties
1950s	.25	4
1960s	.273	7
1970s	.273	0
1980s	.231	2
1990s	.231	0
2000s	.846	13
2010s	**1.10**	**53**
2018	**1.10**	**79**

tion." This economic partnership agreement was designed to deal with new challenges and opportunities resulting from globalization, provide access to new markets, contribute to expanding trade and investment, and enhance the mutual ties between India and Japan. It also reiterated the commitment of both states to economic liberalization and sustainable economic development, social development, and environmental protection. Fourteen subsequent treaties are nested within this agreement, making it the most central to the bilateral relationship. This also suggests that economic cooperation remains the pillar of Indo-Japanese cooperation.

Joint Statement between India and Japan on the Occasion of the Fourth Meeting of the Japan India Energy Dialogue (Treaty Number INDJPN24 in fig. 13): This joint statement between the diplomats of India and Japan "recognized the need to facilitate cooperation between the industries of the two countries in order to expand bilateral energy cooperation on a commercial basis" and secured cooperation in the sectors of energy conservation, coal and electricity, renewable energy, and oil and natural gas. The 2010 statement also established a working group to facilitate cooperation in nuclear energy, recognizing the importance of nuclear energy in meeting the energy demands of both countries. Thirteen subsequent bilateral treaties are nested within this agreement, suggesting that (nuclear) energy cooperation is one of the primary areas of cooperation between India and Japan.

Joint Statement by Prime Minister Dr. Manmohan Singh and Prime Minister Dr. Yukio Hatoyama on New Stage of India-Japan Strategic and Global Partnership (Treaty Number INDJPN22 in fig. 13): This agreement signed in 2009 is also a joint statement by the prime ministers of both countries, reiterating the India-Japan global and strategic partnership. This agreement expressed the importance of Japanese official development assistance toward poverty eradication, infrastructure development, tacking environmental concerns, and human resource development in India. Several individual projects covering a wide range of industries were listed within the document.

Joint Statement Vision for India Japan Strategic and Global Partnership in the Next Decade (Treaty Number INDJPN32 in fig. 13): This joint statement concluded the negotiation of an India Japan Comprehensive Economic Partnership Agreement aimed at boosting trade and investment between the two countries. The statement also discusses cooperation on nuclear energy; Japan's investment in boosting India's infrastructure, including smart cities; and common challenges such as terrorism. The two leaders also discussed cultural linkages and academic people-to-people exchanges between India and Japan. They reaffirmed their commitment to the East Asia Summit as well as to ensuring Afghanistan's transition to a stable, democratic state. They also reaffirmed their resolve to address UN reforms, climate change negotiations, and the complete elimination of all nuclear weapons.

India and Japan Vision 2025 Special Strategic and Global Partnership Working Together for Peace and Prosperity of the Indo Pacific Region and the World (INDJPN61 in fig. 13): This 2015 agreement seeks to transform the Indo-Japanese strategic and global partnership into a deep, broad, and action-oriented partnership, with an emphasis on economic cooperation, infrastructure development, and sustainable development. A large number of issues were recognized as avenues for cooperation including transfer of defense technology from Japan to India, US-Japan-India trilateral talks, and India's participation in US Malabar naval exercises, which would provide additional capabilities to address challenges in the Indo-Pacific region. In addition to security led cooperation, the agreement also reiterated that the two countries shared values and common cultural traditions including Buddhism and the "ideals of democracy, tolerance, pluralism and open society." The two leaders also reiterated their commitment to a "peaceful, open, equitable, stable, and rule-based order in the Indo-Pacific region and beyond." Issues such as terrorism, reform of the United Nations, and strengthening regional institutions received special mention within the document, seeking to showcase their priorities.

Joint Statement on the Advancement of the Strategic and Global Partnership between India and Japan (Treaty Number INDJPN20 in fig. 13): This joint statement also addresses a number of issues that are salient for both states including cooperation in the economic, security, academic, and cultural sectors.

Agreement between India and Japan for Cooperation in the Peaceful Uses of Nuclear Energy (Treaty Number INDJPN71 in fig. 13): This agreement sets out the conditions under which both states will cooperate in the development and use of peaceful nuclear energy including the exchange of scientific information, supply of nuclear material, equipment and technology, and the provision of services on matters related to design, construction, support of operation, maintenance of material/equipment within the scope of the agreement.

Analysis and Implications

Based on the information provided in table 14, India and Japan cooperate over a wide range of issues. The issues most central to their bilateral relationship are economic cooperation including trade and investment, energy cooperation including nuclear energy, scientific and technological exchange, and a desire to balance against the rise of China. In addition to this, the two states also cooperate on issue such as health care, education, environment, transportation and communication, and outer space exploration. The network map (fig. 13) suggests that there are various subnetworks significant to the relationship: economic cooperation, nuclear energy cooperation, and strategic cooperation that spell out their joint vision of a peaceful and prosperous Asia.

As described above, while the two states have always sought to cooperate with each other, their treaty patterns witnessed a large increase after 2010 (as described in table 14). In fact, a majority of the treaties in this bilateral relationship (53) were negotiated and have entered into force between 2010 and the present. This suggests that the pace of cooperation between India and Japan has dramatically increased in the past decade, which also witnessed the rise of China as a global power. China's policies and actions in the South China Sea have also become more aggressive in this time period. China's Belt and Road Initiative seeks to connect old trade routes between Asia, the Middle East, and Europe. However, infrastructure projects related to this initiative are seen as a form of extending China's influence and control over a large part of the continent and beyond. This has naturally united India and Japan and brought them closer together to balance the rise of Chinese hegemony in Asia as well as globally. Both states seek a multipolar system and prefer a multilateral approach to addressing regional and global concerns. As democratic states, India and Japan seek to build a rules-based system in Asia as well as to strengthen regional institutions that can set standards for behavior, monitor compliance to mutually agreed upon rules, arbitrate and settle disputes between states and other parties, enable and encourage trade and investment, and strengthen overall cooperation between states in the region

(*India and Japan Vision 2025 Special Strategic and Global Partnership Working Together for Peace and Prosperity of the Indo Pacific Region and the World, 2015*). Many of the lodestone treaties in this relationship are focused on economic ties including trade, investment, aid, and collaboration on infrastructure projects. India and Japan cooperate over a range of issues. Thus, while balancing the rise of China has served as a catalyst in enhancing Indo-Japanese cooperation, their ties are not limited to containing the rise of Chinese hegemony and aggression in the region. As discussed above in their joint statement, both states seek to advance the status of the region, resulting in an Asia first strategy. Since treaties serve as signals of a state's intention toward other states in the international system as well as their foreign policy preferences, both India and Japan have avoided overtly mentioning China as an aggressor or rival in their joint statements.

Conclusion

An in-depth analysis of the Indo-Japanese treaties provides insights on the nature as well as the future of this relationship. India and Japan have been natural allies and friends given the similarity in their political systems, their shared cultural linkages in the form of Buddhism, and the potential for economic exchange given the complementary nature of their markets. More recently, they have a common desire to prevent China's aggressive actions and policies in the Indo-Pacific region. The two states have forged close ties by creating opportunities for cooperation over a wide range of issues. The issues most central to their efforts at cooperation are economic interactions including trade and investment, scientific and technological cooperation, and energy cooperation (including nuclear energy). In addition to treaty formation, India and Japan have created a number of opportunities for cooperation, such as elevating their bilateral relationship to the level of a strategic and global partnership, including summit level meetings annually and cooperating via Asian regional institutions such as the Association of Southeast Asian Nations (ASEAN). India and Japan do not overtly mention balancing the rise of China as their primary goal in any of their bilateral treaties. However, as noted above, the *India and Japan Vision 2025 Special Strategic and Global Partnership Working Together for Peace and Prosperity of the Indo Pacific Region and the World* clearly outlines their vision for a "peaceful, open, equitable, stable and rule-based order in the Indo-Pacific region and beyond." Although India's nonaligned policy has prevented it from forming a security alliance with Japan, both states are continuing to bolster security cooperation by conducting a number of joint military exercises that also include additional states such as the United States and Australia. Thus, India and Japan have walked a fine line in signaling their intentions to cooperate and balance the rise of China without any overt threats or aggression toward China. They have invested in a multitude of areas to ensure that they are prepared to contain Chinese aggression in the region.

Part 3 • India's Relationship with Revisionist Powers

7 • Indo-Russian Relations

An Overview of the Relationship

Despite massive losses, the Soviet Union was one of only two states that were powerful enough to survive World War II as a great power. While the Soviet Union and the United States had been allies during World War II, once the conflict ended, a new era of competition emerged between the two distinct ideologies. On the one hand, the United States believed in liberalism and capitalism. The Soviet Union, on the other hand, believed in communism. Both of those ideologies were in direct conflict and created an ideological battlefield where the two states competed for superiority.

The invention of the atomic bomb by the United States heralded a new age where conventional war gave way to the possibility of nuclear holocaust. The Soviet Union was quick to recognize the power of the atomic bomb and worked to create its own nuclear program. While the United States was technically more powerful than the Soviet Union, nevertheless the Red Army had captured a large part of Eastern Europe and had numerical superiority over American troops stationed in Europe.

This Cold War era, as it came to be known, was bipolar. Both the Soviet Union and the United States did not fight each other directly, but via proxy wars between their allies. For example, the Soviet Union supported the North Vietnamese and the United States fought with the South Vietnamese in the Vietnam War. Similarly, in Afghanistan, the United States supported the Mujahedeen, which actively fought against the Soviet Union.

During the Cold War, Europe was essentially partitioned between the United States and the Soviet Union. The Soviet Union controlled much of Eastern Europe, establishing puppet governments that also served as buffer states from future potential attacks from the West. The Soviet Union also controlled East Germany and East Berlin. The United States and its allies remained in Western Europe, with Germany being partitioned between East and West. The Soviet Union established the Warsaw Pact as a collective security organization to ensure the security of the Soviet Union and its allies in Europe. The United States and its allies established NATO. Both organizations were responsible for protecting their member states from attack by the other organizations' member states.

In the rest of the world, the Soviet Union and the United States competed for influence among the other powers. For example, in East Asia, Japan allied itself with the United States while China initially allied itself with the Soviet Union. Similarly, in South Asia, India was closer to the Soviet Union while Pakistan allied itself with the United States. Despite the fact that India officially remained nonaligned, for all intents and purposes it maintained close ties with the Soviet Union.

The collapse of the Soviet Union allowed a reset to occur in India's foreign policy. It could build a new relationship with both Russia and the United States. Russia, as the successor state to the Soviet Union, agreed to abide by all of the previous treaties signed by the Soviet Union. However, Moscow also realized that it needed to develop a new relationship with New Delhi that was less ideologically driven and geared more toward mutual cooperation.

Despite the fact that Russia was a much weaker state than the Soviet Union had been, Russia still inherited nuclear weapons as well as a very powerful defense industry from the Soviet Union. Russia also developed expertise in space exploration including its involvement in the International Space Station. Thus, there were avenues of cooperation between Moscow and New Delhi. However, New Delhi also had traded with the United States during the Cold War and wanted to improve its relations with the United States in the post–Cold War era.

In this chapter, we first examine the relationship between Moscow and New Delhi, taking into account the historical relationship between both states. We then turn to analysis of the relationship through the use of treaty networks to determine the quality of the relationship between the two states and more specifically whether or not the two states have an institutionalized relationship. If India is a status quo power, we would expect there to be ad hoc cooperation between India and Russia. In contrast, if India is a revisionist power, we should see evidence of institutionalized cooperation between the two states.

Indo-Russian Ties

India and Russia have developed a special and privileged partnership. In 2019, Russian President Vladimir Putin bestowed the highest state decoration of Russia—the Order of St Andrew the Apostle—on Indian prime minister Narendra Modi for "his distinguished contribution to the development of a privileged strategic partnership between Russia and India and friendly ties between the Russian and Indian people" (Dipanjan 2019).

Indo-Russian ties have been very close since the start of the bilateral relationship.[1] While remaining nonaligned, India maintained close ties with the Soviet Union throughout the Cold War. While it was leaning toward the Soviets, India also accepted aid from and conducted trade with the United States as well as with European powers. In 1971, India and the Soviet Union signed a Treaty of Friendship that further enhanced their relationship.

Russia has been India's largest arms supplier and has also provided India with much-needed support on the global stage on sensitive issues such as Kashmiri independence and India's decision to become a nuclear weapons state. Not only did Russia not condemn India's actions in the above situations but also blocked UN Security Council resolutions aimed against India, which were often initiated by the United States and supported by France and the United Kingdom.[2] As a result, the Soviet Union/Russia has proven to be a long-term reliable ally to India. More recently, Russia has supported India's abrogation of Article 370 of its constitution, thus revoking the special autonomy status of Jammu and Kashmir. India also suspended the statehood of Jammu and Kashmir and instituted a communications blackout to prevent riots, backlash, and violence in the region. While these actions were severely condemned by countries around the world, Russia has remained supportive of India's domestic policy. Russia has also expressed support for India's assertion that the dispute over Kashmir should be handled bilaterally between India and Pakistan without the interference of external actors. India has also refused to condemn Russia's actions in Ukraine or participate in international sanctions against the country. The two states have rarely criticized each other's policies in public, thus providing each other unequivocal support on the global stage. In 2000, India and Russia elevated their relationship to a strategic partnership and have continued to hold annual bilateral summit-level meetings between the leaders of the two states.[3]

After the collapse of the Soviet Union in 1991, India contributed to the revival of the Russian defense industry by continuing to purchase heavy military equipment from Russian firms. Russia provided India with sensitive and

---

1. For a detailed account of Indo-Russian ties through history, see Budhwar (2007) and Kundu (2008).

2. Dipanjan (2019).

3. Declaration of Strategic Partnership between the Republic of India and the Russian Federation, October 3, 2000. India Bilateral Treaties and Agreements. Retrieved from Ministry of External Affairs India: https://mea.gov.in/TreatyList.htm?1

advanced equipment that the United States and other countries were unwilling to provide. Russia has helped India acquire nuclear-propelled submarines and a military aircraft carrier; it has also provided assistance in building the Brahmos supersonic anti-ship and land attack missile.[4]

While India has diversified its arms procurement system by also purchasing from the United States, France, and Israel, a majority of India's defense systems remain Russian based. The path dependency generated due to the heavy investment that India has already made in Russian-based defense systems suggests that India is unlikely to abandon existing systems and change to American-based defense systems in the near future. India seeks to continue to import the latest military technology from Russia since the United States has been unwilling to share sensitive technology or to provide certain types of advanced weapons to India.[5] It is worth noting that a majority of the defense systems of Pakistan (which remains India's top rival) are American manufactured. It is therefore also unlikely that the United States will be sharing the same equipment and technology with India. India and Russia have also formed agreements to undertake the joint production of military equipment, in support of the "Make in India" campaign.

India and Russia have been involved in several joint military exercises as well: the tri-services exercise INDRA and Russia's Tsentr military exercises (which India was first invited to in 2019) are annual exercises in the Indo-Pacific.[6] The two countries have attempted to enhance cultural ties including joint educational programs, student exchanges, and language skills.[7]

India and Russia continue to cooperate in multilateral forums including the UN, the Shanghai Cooperation Organization, the BRICS, the Russia-India-China informal grouping, and so forth. The two sides have held annual summit-level meetings that have alternated between India and Russia starting in 2000. In addition to joint annual summits, leaders of the two countries often hold summit-level meetings on the sidelines of other global forums such as the G-20 and the Shanghai Cooperation Organization.[8]

---

4. India Russia Relations, Ministry of External Affairs, http://mea.gov.in/Portal/Foreign-Relation/India_Russia_May.pdf

5. Cara Abercrombie, "Removing Barriers to US-India Defense Trade," Carnegie Endowment for International Peace, January 10, 2018. https://carnegieendowment.org/2018/01/10/removing-barriers-to-u.s.-india-defense-trade-pub-75206

6. Press Information Bureau, "Curtain Raiser—Ex Tsentr 2019," https://pib.gov.in/PressReleasePage.aspx?PRID=1584258 (accessed November 9, 2019).

7. Ministry of External Affairs, "Indian Students Studying in Foreign Countries," https://data.gov.in/resources/country-wise-indian-students-studying-abroad-december-2020-ministry-external-affairs (accessed March 10, 2022).

8. "India-Russia Relations," May 2017, http://mea.gov.in/Portal/ForeignRelation/India_Russia_May.pdf

The biggest impediment to stronger ties between India and Russia is their lack of meaningful trade outside of the defense sector.[9] Indo-Russian trade remains at around 1 percent of their overall trade.[10] Total bilateral trade between India and Russia in 2016 amounted to US$ 7.71billion (this was a decline of 1.5% from 2015). Total bilateral trade is 2017 was US$10.17 billion; in 2018 it was US$11 billion.[11] India-Russia trade, while low, has remained consistent. In September 2019, the leaders of the two countries pledged to triple bilateral trade to US$30 billion by 2025.[12] While both countries have repeatedly discussed and attempted to increase trade in nondefense areas, it has not materialized. However, the two states have increased investment in each other's economy. Russia has invited India to invest in the Russian Far East (RFE); Indian delegations comprising business associations and politicians have identified diamond cutting, petrochemicals, wood processing, and tourism as potential areas of interest for Indian investment in the RFE.[13] Energy is also a key area of economic cooperation between the two countries. Mutual investments between India and Russia are at approximately $11 billion currently, with both sides promising to increase investments to $30–$50 billion by 2025 (Volodin 2017). Heavy sanctions placed on Russia by the West in the aftermath of the 2015 Ukraine crisis may further enhance India's value as a market for Russian products and as a destination for Russian investments. Prime Minister Modi's "Make in India" initiative will provide additional opportunities for Russian industries to invest in Indian economy sectors such as civil aviation, defense equipment, and railways (Volodin 2017).

Both India and Russia are wary of the emergence of a bipolar global order led by the United States and China, which would reduce the space for strategic maneuverability for both countries. Thus, it is crucial for the leaders of both countries to reinvent and reinvigorate the Indo-Russian relationship (Kaura 2019). India is also concerned about the growing closeness between Russia and China. However, many scholars argue that the Russian-Chinese relationship is an alliance of convenience (Kaura 2019). In the realm of eco-

9. Nivedita Kapoor, "India-Russia Relations: Beyond Energy and Defence," Observer Research Foundation *Issue Brief No. 327*, December 2019.

10. Russia Direct, "How to Take Russia-India Economic Ties to the Next Level," https://russia-direct.org/opinion/how-take-russia-india-economic-ties-next-level (accessed October 25, 2019).

11. Nivedita Kapoor 2019.

12. Sudha Ramachandran, "What's India Doing in Russia's Far East," *Diplomat*, October 19, 2019, https://thediplomat.com/2019/10/whats-india-doing-in-russias-far-east/

13. Ministry of External Affairs, "Visit of Deputy Prime Minister of Russia to India," https://mea.gov.in/press-releases.htm?dtl/31453/visit+of+deputy+ (accessed September 26, 2019).

nomic power, multiple poles of power have emerged with the balance of power system back in place. We see India and Russia engaging in economic cooperation, both to balance the United States and China and to prevent any one state becoming the hegemonic power (Volodin 2017).

Russia's ties with the West have severely deteriorated since Russia's annexation of Crimea in 2014. While the EU remains one of Russia's largest trading partners, heavy American sanctions as well as falling oil prices have stagnated the Russian economy and its ability to wield influence in Eastern Europe, Central Asia, and beyond. Russia has increasingly turned to China as a source of investment in the far eastern part of the country and has become its top oil supplier. However, given the power imbalance between Russia and China, Russia has increased its bilateral cooperation with India for two crucial reasons. First, India serves to counterbalance China's power and dominance in Asia.[14] Second, given the background of American sanctions, Russia wants to solidify ties with eastern middle powers such as China and India to avoid economic and political isolation and to attempt to revise the global economic order.

India's interest in the Russian Far East is driven partially by economic interests and partially by strategic interests. In addition to enhancing India's role in RFE development, the two countries are also exploring the viability and efficiency of the Chennai-Vladivostok sea route, which will halve the time and distance to Russia compared to the Suez Canal route through Europe.[15] Such a route would also increase India's presence in the Chinese-dominated South China Sea and counter China's efforts to build the Belt and Road Initiative. Currently, China accounts for two-thirds of the investment in the RFE while India has extended a $1 billion line of credit for development in the RFE.[16]

---

14. Roy Chaudhary Dipanjan, "Russia Seeks to Balance China in Far East; Woos Indian Investments," *Economic Times*, July 24, 2019, https://economictimes.indiatimes.com/news/defence/russia-seeks-to-balance-china-in-far-east-woos-indian-investments/articleshow/70366045.cms?from=mdr

15. "Translation of Prime Minister's Speech in Plenary Session of 5th Eastern Economic Forum," September 5, 2019, https://mea.gov.in/Speeches-Statements.htm?dtl/31798/Translation_of_Prime_Ministers_speech_in_Plenary_Session_of_5th_Eastern_Economic_Forum_September_05_2019

16. Roy Chaudhary Dipanjan, "Russia Seeks to Balance China in Far East; Woos Indian Investments," *Economic Times*, July 24, 2019, https://economictimes.indiatimes.com/news/defence/russia-seeks-to-balance-china-in-far-east-woos-indian-investments/articleshow/70366045.cms?from=mdr

Disagreements in the Relationship

The growing cooperation and the formation of a strategic partnership between India and the United States has the potential to destabilize Indo-Russian ties but so far that has not happened. The United States has also become a major arms supplier to India, and threatens to replace Russia as India's largest defense supplier. In this chapter, we argue that Indo-Russian ties are deeply institutionalized and unlikely to be altered in the near future. However, in retaliation for India's growing cooperation with the United States, Russia has lifted an arms embargo over Pakistan and has chosen to enter into a defense trade with Pakistan.[17] Russia and Pakistan have also engaged in joint military exercises. India protested against the growing closeness between Russia and Pakistan and expressed its discontent at Russia sharing the same class of weapons with Pakistan that had also been sold to India, thus undermining India's military advantage over Pakistan.[18] In response to this, Russia scaled back its defense trade with Pakistan.[19] However, Russia continues to supply arms to both Pakistan and China, which remain India's largest rivals.

The Russia-China relationship is growing increasingly cooperative. The two countries have engaged in joint military exercises including the first ever joint air patrol of the South China Sea.[20] Russia is also providing China with modern weaponry. Hence it remains in India's best interest to maintain close ties with Russia and continue to collaborate with Russia on defense-related matters so as to balance China's military advantage.

In this chapter, we analyze Indo-Russian ties by studying the pattern of bilateral treaty formation between the two countries. We first study the type and number of treaties concluded between the two countries. Next, we study patterns of treaty nesting or ties between individual treaties that link them to one another. Then we present information on lodestone treaties that are crucial to the relationship. And we analyze the findings and their implications

17. Iwanek Kryzstof, "Russia's Looming Arms Sale to Pakistan Sets Up a Dangerous Game," *The Diplomat*, May 2019, https://thediplomat.com/2019/05/russias-looming-arms-sale-to-pakistan-sets-up-a-dangerous-game/

18. Kryzstof, "Russia's Looming Arms Sale to Pakistan Sets Up a Dangerous Game."

19. Snehesh Alex Phillip, "Russia Rejects Pakistan Request for 50,000 AK Rifles, Assures India of No Deals in Future," *Print*, July 17, 2019, https://theprint.in/defence/russia-rejects-pakistan-request-for-50000-ak-rifles-assures-india-of-no-deals-in-future/264004/

20. Franz-Stefan Gady, "China, Russia Conduct First Ever Joint Strategic Bomber Patrol Flights in Indo-Pacific Region," *The Diplomat*, July 23, 2019, https://thediplomat.com/2019/07/china-russia-conduct-first-ever-joint-strategic-bomber-patrol-flights-in-indo-pacific-region/

for the future of the Indo-Russian relationship. We find a high level of treaty nesting in the Indo-Russian treaty network, suggesting that the relationship is deeply institutionalized and unlikely to deteriorate in the near future. We conclude by discussing the implications of these findings for India's future alignment patterns.

Indo-Russian Treaty Network

To analyze the strength of the Indo-Russian bilateral relationship, we study three metrics: the total number of treaties in the Indo-Russian treaty network, the range of issues over which the two countries cooperate, and the cooperation score resulting from treaty nesting in the network.

India and Russia have signed a total of 217 bilateral treaties from 1947 to 2018. Thus, there are a higher number of treaties present in the Indo-Russian relationship compared to the Indo-US bilateral network. Table 16 presents information on the type of treaties created within this relationship.

India and Russia have signed a large number of treaties over a large range of issues. The two countries have created 64 treaties on issues related to cooperation.[21] The broad category of cooperation includes treaties that discuss peace, friendship, and the formation of a strategic partnership between the two countries. It also includes treaties that discuss their joint vision for the global hierarchy, the global economy, and Asia. Some of these treaties serve as the foundation over which the bilateral relationship is built. As we discuss in later sections of this chapter, several treaties make explicit reference to the Treaty of Peace, Friendship and Cooperation (1971) as well as the Treaty of Friendship and Cooperation (1993).

The second highest number of treaties is on issues related to science and technology (30), followed by trade (23), economic and technical assistance (18), energy (15), and space cooperation (14). In addition to this, the two states cooperate on a number of other issues (see table 16). This is in stark contrast to the extent of cooperation that exists between India and the United States.

As depicted in figure 14, the Indo-Russian treaty map is extremely dense with a high number of ties between the treaties. There are very few isolated treaties in the network; most treaties are connected to at least one other treaty and several treaties are connected to two or more treaties. As the treaty

---

21. While this is a broad category, the issue areas are provided by the Government of India's Ministry of External Affairs.

Table 16. Indo-Russian Treaties, 1947–2019

Issues	Number of Treaties
Cooperation	64
Science and Technology	30
Trade	23
Economic and Technical Assistance	18
Energy	15
Space Cooperation	14
Education	6
Air Travel	6
Agriculture	4
Drug Trafficking	3
Tourism	3
Oil	3
Terrorism	3
Investment	2
Environment	2
Legal Assistance	1
Crime	1
Health	1
Transfer of Prisoners	1
Communication	1
Audio Video Coproduction	1
Currency Rate	1
Taxation	1

map in figure 14 demonstrates, there is an extremely high degree of treaty nesting within the Indo-Russian bilateral relationship.

Table 17 presents information on the evolution of the cooperation score in the Indo-Russian relationship. As discussed in the methodology section, the cooperation score within a bilateral relationship is measured by dividing the total number of treaties with the total number of ties in a relationship (Slobodchikoff 2013). A score of less than 1 suggests ad hoc cooperation and a score greater than 1 suggests institutionalized cooperation (Slobodchikoff 2013). The cooperation score between India and Russia crosses the threshold of 1 in 2010 as the total number of ties surpasses the total number of treaties. This Indo-Russian relationship is currently in the phase of institutionalized cooperation as the cooperation score remains greater than 1. Below, we discuss the treaty network map as well as the key treaties in the relationship.

Table 18 presents all the lodestone treaties in the Indo-Russian treaty network in their order of importance. Below we discuss each of these lodestone treaties in depth.

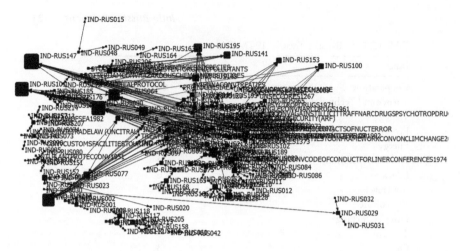

Fig. 14. Indo-Russia Treaty Network

Table 17. Indo-Russian Bilateral Cooperation Score

Year	Treaties	Ties	Cooperation Score
1950	0	0	0
1960	12	8	.6667
1970	35	15	.4375
1980	58	38	.5926
1990	65	39	.6094
2000	107	70	.654
2010	176	189	**1.074**
2018	217	236	**1.09**

Table 18. Lodestone Treaties in the Indo-Russian Treaty Network

Treaty Number	Name	Number of Ties
IND-RUS147	Joint Declaration between India and Russia	16.00
IND-RUS090	Declaration of Strategic Partnership between India and Russian Federation	14.00
IND-RUS114	Agreement between India and Russia on Cooperation in the Exploration and Use of Outer Space	13.00
IND-RUS064	Treaty of Friendship and Cooperation between India and Russia	11.00
IND-RUS107	Declaration between India and Russia on Global Challenges and Threats to World Security	9.00
IND-RUS195	Strategic Vision for Strengthening Cooperation in Peaceful Uses of Atomic Energy between India and Russia	8.00
IND-RUS036	Treaty of Peace, Friendship and Cooperation between India and Russia	7.00

- *The Joint Declaration between India and Russia* (IND-RUS147 in fig. 14) was signed in 2008. It has 16 ties with other treaties in the network; it is nested within 5 bilateral treaties and 11 multilateral treaties. This treaty is nested within the ASEAN Regional Forum on Security, Asia Cooperation Dialogue, UN Security Council Resolution 1737, UN Security Council Resolution 1747, UN Security Council Resolution 1803, UN Security Council Resolution 1835, UN Security Council Resolution 242, UN Security Council Resolution 338, UN Security Council Resolution 1397, UN Security Council Resolution 1515; and the Annapolis Conference. In addition to this, it is also nested within 5 bilateral Indo-Russian treaties including the Treaty of Friendship and Cooperation between India and Russia (1993); Declaration on Strategic Partnership between India and Russian Federation (2000); Protocol between India and Russia on Holding "Year of Russia in India" in the Year 2008 and "Year of India in Russia" in the Year 2009 (2007); Agreement between the Government of the Republic of India and the Government of the Russian Federation on Reciprocal Protection of Intellectual Property Rights on the Field of Military–Technical Cooperation (2005); and Agreement between India and Russia on Cooperation to Combat Illicit Trafficking in Narcotics, Psychotropic Substances and Their Precursors (2007).
- The *Declaration of Strategic Partnership between India and Russian Federation* (IND-RUS090 in fig. 14) was signed in 2000 and is nested within four previous bilateral treaties. It has 14 ties within the network; 10 subsequent Indo-Russian bilateral treaties reference this declaration and are nested within it. The declaration is nested within the Treaty of Peace, Friendship and Cooperation between India and Russia (1971), Treaty of Friendship and Cooperation between India and Russia (1993), an Intergovernmental Agreement (1992), and the Moscow Declaration on the Protection of the Interests of Pluralistic States (1994).
- *Agreement between India and Russia on Cooperation in the Exploration and Use of Outer Space* (IND-RUS114 in fig. 14) was signed in 2004. It has 13 ties within the treaty network; it is nested within two bilateral Indo-Russian treaties—the Agreement between India and Russian on Co-Operation in the Exploration and Use of Outer Space for Peaceful Purposes (1994) and the Agreement on the Protection of Confidential Materials (2000)—as well as one multilateral treaty, the Convention on International Liability on Damage Caused by Space Objects (1972). Ten subsequent bilateral Indo-Russian treaties are nested within this

agreement on cooperation in the exploration and use of outer space. As depicted in table 16, India and Russia have signed a total of 14 treaties on space exploration, most of which are connected to, or nested within, each other.

- *Treaty of Friendship and Cooperation between India and Russia* (IND-RUS064 in fig. 14) was signed in 1993. It has 11 ties to other treaties within the network. It is nested within the Treaty of Peace, Friendship and Cooperation between India and Russia (1971). Ten subsequent bilateral Indo-Russian treaties are nested within this agreement.

- *Declaration between India and Russia on Global Challenges and Threats to World Security* (IND-RUS107 in fig. 14) was signed in 2003. It is nested within the Treaty of Friendship and Cooperation between India and Russia (1993), the Declaration of Strategic Partnership between India and Russian Federation (2000), the Moscow Declaration on the Protection of the Interests of Pluralistic States (1994), the Moscow Declaration between India and Russian Federation on International Terrorism (2001), the MOU between India and Russia on Cooperation in Combating Terrorism (2002), and the Delhi Declaration on Further Consolidation of Strategic Partnership between India and Russia (2002). It is also nested within the following multilateral agreements: the United Nations Millennium Declaration, United Nations Resolution 57/145, UN Resolution 1373, and the Bonn Agreement.

- *Strategic Vision for Strengthening Cooperation in Peaceful Uses of Atomic Energy between India and Russia* (IND-RUS195 in fig. 14) was signed in 2014. It is nested within the Treaty of Friendship and Cooperation between India and Russia (1993); the Agreement between India and USSR on Cooperation in the Construction of a Nuclear Power Station in India (1988); the MOU between India and Russia concerning Broader Scientific and Technical Cooperation in the Field of Peaceful Uses of Nuclear Energy (2010); the MOU between India and Russia on Cooperation in Information Technology (2010); the Agreement between the Government of Republic of India and the Government of Russian Federation on Cooperation in the Use of Atomic Energy for Peaceful Purposes (2010); and the General Framework Agreement for KKNPP (Kudankulam Nuclear Power Plant) (2014).

- *Treaty of Peace, Friendship and Cooperation between India and Russia* (IND-RUS036 in fig. 14) was signed in 1971. It is nested within the Trade Agreement on Trade between India and Russia (1970).

There are several other treaties in the treaty network with five or six ties. As a point of comparison, there is not a single treaty in the Indo-US relation that has more than four ties to other treaties in the network.

Institutionalization of Ties—Analysis

As mentioned earlier in this chapter, regular annual summit-level meetings alternating between India and Russia have been held between the leaders of the two countries starting in 2000. A large number of bilateral agreements are typically signed at these summit-level meetings, ranging from weapons procurement to trade and investment. About 50 business agreements were signed at the 2019 EEF summit level meeting between Prime Minister Modi and President Putin. It is a fair criticism that India does not always follow through on agreements concluded and signed by its leaders. Often a lack of resources or a change in priorities by a new administration leads to a policy shift. However, Indian policy vis-à-vis Russia has not seen a dramatic shift in spite of changes in the administration and leadership. Given the sheer magnitude of agreements concluded between the two countries, even a small proportion of them leading to concrete actions would result in several points of cooperation between the two countries.

Various ministerial-level bilateral visits are also held between the two states. Two Inter-Governmental Commissions—one dealing with trade and scientific cooperation, and another on military cooperation—meet annually. The Inter-Governmental Commission on Military Technical Cooperation co-chaired by the Ministers of Defense of Russia and India also review defense cooperation between the two countries regularly.[22]

In reference to Indo-Russian ties, India's Ministry of External Affairs states, "India has longstanding and wide-ranging cooperation with Russia in the field of defence. India-Russia military technical cooperation has evolved from a buyer-seller framework to one involving joint research, development and production of advanced defence technologies and systems. BrahMos Missile System as well as the licensed production in India of SU-30 aircraft and T-90 tanks, are examples of such flagship cooperation."[23]

Russia has assisted India in building its first nuclear power plant and the

---

22. See https://mea.gov.in/Portal/ForeignRelation/Russia_unclassified_bilateral_brief_January_2013.pdf

23. "India-Russia Relations," May 2017, http://mea.gov.in/Portal/ForeignRelation/India_Russia_May.pdf

two countries are cooperating to build several more nuclear power plants in India. India and Russia are also cooperating to build a nuclear power plant in Bangladesh.[24] In addition to this, India and Russia are also looking to cooperate to build nuclear power plants across third party states in Africa and the Middle East.[25]

India's first satellite, *Aryabhatt*, launched into space with the help of a Russian *Soyuz* capsule from a Soviet space station in 1975. In 2007, the two countries signed a Framework Agreement on Cooperation in Peaceful Uses of Outer Space. "In 2015, the space agencies in both countries signed an MOU on the expansion of cooperation in the field of the exploration and use of outer space for peaceful purposes. An agreement was signed between C-DAC and GLONASS for cooperation in technologies based on satellite navigation. On 15 October 2016, ISRO and Roscosmos signed an MOU to establish ground measurement gathering stations for GLONASS and NavIC in India and Russia. Both sides are also exploring the possibility of cooperation in manned space flight."[26] Russia is currently assisting India in its maiden human space mission, Gaganyaan.[27]

In addition to the above, several people-to-people initiatives—various efforts to deeply institutionalize ties—are conducted by the governments in both states.[28]

Conclusion

The strength of India-Russia ties lies in the scope and magnitude of their defense ties and the desire of both countries to establish a multipolar global order. The disagreements between the two powers are insubstantial and can

24. Roy Choudhary Dipanjan, "India, Russia, Bangladesh Sign Tripartite Pact for Civil Nuclear Cooperation," *Economic Times*, March 1, 2018, https://economictimes.indiatimes .com/news/defence/india-russia-bangladesh-sign-tripartite-pact-for-civil-nuclear-cooperati on/articleshow/63127669.cms

25. Palash Ghosh, "Russia, India May Cooperate to Build Nuclear Plants in Middle East, Africa," *IB Times*, February 9, 2020, https://www.ibtimes.com/russia-india-may-cooperate- build-nuclear-plants-middle-east-africa-2918741

26. "India-Russia Relations," May 2017, http://mea.gov.in/Portal/ForeignRelation/ India_Russia_May.pdf

27. "India, Russia Hold Talks to Boost Space Cooperation," *Indian Express*, July 12, 2019, https://indianexpress.com/article/india/india-russia-hold-talks-to-boost-space-cooperation -5827059/

28. "India-Russia Relations," May 2017, http://mea.gov.in/Portal/ForeignRelation/ India_Russia_May.pdf

be addressed by continued diplomatic efforts by leaders on both sides. The two countries have remained close allies and have offered each other unwavering support on the global stage, especially in times of crises. The changing nature of global polarity brought about by the rise of China and the decline of American power will require India and Russia to rejuvenate their ties.

India and Russia have expended a lot of resources (including human resources) toward the development of their strategic partnership. The two countries consult on a wide range of issues and often are on the same side in multilateral forums such as the BRICS, the G-20, and the United Nations. The relationship is marked by trust on both sides to stand by each other and to refrain from criticizing each other's domestic and foreign policies in a public forum. While this bilateral relationship is largely driven by defense and security, the two countries have made efforts to boost trade and investment in each other's economy. More importantly, they have also created a framework of cooperation by creating a series of agreements, several of which are nested within each other. This has led to deeply institutionalized ties that are likely to withstand changing global hierarchies and shifts in global power. The Indo-Russian relationship is unlikely to weaken in the near future. Given the analysis in this chapter, we expect it to remain stable and strong.

India and Russia maintain a strong institutionalized bilateral relationship. Both states have discussed at various times the need to move from a unilateral global order to a multilateral global order. While India believes this, as we have seen in the previous section of the book, India has continued to maintain a relationship with the United States and its allies. However, it should be clear that India's relationship with Russia is extremely problematic if the United States needs India's help to maintain the status quo in the current global order. Russia, on the other hand, is in a strong position to convince India to support a change in the global order. The relationship between India and Russia is strong enough that it should only continue to grow stronger. The window to woo India away from a strong relationship with Russia and to entice it to become a solid status quo power has closed. Contrary to that, Russia has not fully convinced India to completely turn away from a relationship with the United States and its allies. If the relationship between Russia and India grows stronger, however, that is a distinct possibility. To further assess India's preferences in terms of the global order, one must not only examine India's relationship with Russia but also India's relationships with other revisionist powers such as China. In the next chapter we examine India's relationship with China.

8 • Indo-Chinese Relations

It is widely speculated that the global leadership void left behind by the United States will be filled by states like China, Germany, and others. Multilateral institutions and forums such as NATO and the G-20 are adjusting to the current political landscape where the United States seems disinterested in leading and other states are scrambling to maintain stability. States such as Brazil, Russia, India, China, and South Africa (BRICS) and others have long desired a multipolar global order, where they have a larger say in shaping global affairs.

International relations scholars have debated whether or not the current system is unipolar, with the United States acting as a global hegemon. In terms of military power, the United States maintains its global dominance, far outspending its rivals and competitors, thus maintaining the largest and best-equipped armed forces in the world. While the US remains the world's largest economy, it continues to face growing competition from rising powers like China, India, and the European Union.

Increasingly, the United States has been unwilling as well as unable to handle global crises, both economic and security related. It has been unable to thwart North Korea's nuclear proliferation. It has been unable to entirely eliminate the Islamic State and other extremist fundamentalist groups. It has been a reluctant participant in the Syrian civil war, allowing states like Russia and Turkey to take the lead in shaping the situation on the ground. These events point to the United States' lack of global leadership.[1] It can be argued that we are witnessing the transition of global order toward a multipolar sys-

---

1. While the book is a study through 2017, that the US has not been able to achieve victory in Afghanistan, and has showed more global leadership during the Ukraine War, but still has not been able to regain its leadership role that it had at the end of the Cold War.

tem, where a group of major powers jointly govern and shape the rules of the system under which other states must operate.

In previous chapters, we have argued that a state like India could serve as a lynchpin in this transition from unipolarity toward multipolarity. By choosing to side with Russia instead of the United States, India can act as a catalyst in a global transition of power. Current trends point to the increasing cooperation between India and the United States. As the world's largest and leading democracies, they have much in common with each other. It is widely expected that they will continue to cooperate economically, and India will be a crucial ally in the United States' "pivot to" or "rebalancing in" Asia. India and the United States share a common concern for the rise of China and its expanding aggression in Asia-Pacific as well as globally. Much has been written about the close ties developed between the Modi and Obama administrations. Modi and Trump also developed close ties, and the close economic, security, and political cooperation between the two countries is expected to continue. The successful Indian diaspora in the United States provides a crucial connection between the two states. These trends suggest that India is being pulled away from the Russian sphere of influence by the United States and is realigning its foreign policy interests with the US.

However, all of these current analyses ignore the historic nature of the ties between India and China. If India and China have institutionalized cooperation, then it is likely that India is a solidly revisionist state. However, if China and India possess an ad hoc relationship, it might be possible for India to be a status quo power. By analyzing the nature of treaty formation between these dyads, we arrive at the conclusion that India and China do not have a cooperative relationship, but have managed to address areas of mutual concern to avoid short-term conflict.

Challenging US Hegemony

We have discussed the challenge to US hegemony posed by Russia in the previous chapter. Like Moscow, Beijing had its own reasons for challenging US hegemony. By 2010, China had grown into an economic power. The reforms that were instituted by Deng Xiao Ping had effectively created a modified capitalist economy. Interestingly, Beijing learned from Gorbachev's attempted reforms in the Soviet Union, and realized that they would not be successful in reforming both the political and economic systems. They saw that as people got more political freedoms, they began demanding more changes, and this led to the collapse of the Soviet Union.

Instead of following the Soviet reform model, Beijing focused only on economic reforms. They chose not to reform the political system, but continued to maintain a strong hold over the political system.

In 2010, China's economy was the second most powerful economy in the world, surpassing Japan. Beijing dominated trade and began to loan money to several countries, including the United States. China had been increasingly showing signs of becoming dissatisfied with the global order and unipolarity. China had also been challenging the United States in the South China Sea, and had been expanding its influence in regions including Central and South America as well as Africa. Officially, both China and Russia had stated that they favored a multipolar system as opposed to the unipolar system with the United States at its helm. In fact, on May 15, 1997, the Russian and the Chinese permanent UN diplomatic missions presented an official declaration to the United Nations General Assembly of an intent to create a multipolar world and thus create a new international security structure.[2]

Despite using rhetoric claiming that they were in favor of a multipolar system, neither Russia nor China could directly take on US power. They each had to begin to challenge US power at the periphery, such as Moscow orchestrating efforts for Kyrgyzstan to force American troops to leave the Manas Airbase in Kyrgyzstan or Beijing creating new islands in the South China Sea. However, even working together, Moscow and Beijing would not be strong enough to directly challenge US power. They had to work within the confines of existing organizations, such as the Shanghai Cooperation Organization, and convince other countries to join them in an effort to balance against US power to create a multipolar system. The Shanghai Cooperation Organization was a way to manage regional tensions between Beijing and Moscow. The two states began to work together in Central Asia, and while the Shanghai Cooperation Organization did not completely end competition between the great powers, it nevertheless helped manage the competition.

Beijing's Belt and Road Initiative focused on economic expansion and globalization for China. Beijing invested heavily in infrastructure projects in many other states, while not demanding political changes. In other words, the Belt and Road Initiative became a competitor of the International Monetary Fund and the World Bank. In directly competing with these organizations, Beijing provided a distinct choice for states looking to improve their infrastructure. States were attracted to the Belt and Road Initiative because they did not have to make political changes to their regimes. Beijing profited from these arrangements since, instead of requiring political changes, it

---

2. http://www.un.org/documents/ga/docs/52/plenary/a52-153.htm

required states to allow Chinese companies to work on the infrastructure projects, and often used those projects as collateral if the countries could not pay back loans that the Chinese provided. For example, the Chinese accepted the Port of Mombasa as collateral from Kenya for helping to build up the infrastructure of the port.

One of the main countries that Beijing needed to target was India. India was the classic status quo power. Despite having allied itself with Moscow during the Cold War, India had received prominence during both President Bush's and President Obama's presidencies as Washington sought to keep its hegemonic status. The United States also realized that it had to overcome decades of adversarial US foreign policies against India. Both President Bush and President Obama realized that they needed India and its growing economy as an important ally to prevent China and Russia from developing power preponderance and more importantly the ability to challenge the existing global hierarchy.

Russia and China also recognized the importance of India and of gaining India as a valuable ally in countering American hegemony. If there was to be a viable challenge to US hegemony, Moscow and Beijing had to convince India that it needed to ally itself with them. Beginning in 2002, the leaders of the three states have held annual summits to increase their cooperation. In fact, the tripartite meetings in 2017 reiterated that all three states were interested in creating a global system based on international law and moving toward a multipolar system.[3]

While India very much prefers the status quo, it also has a lifelong penchant for multilateralism (which first began under the leadership of Nehru as independent India's first prime minister). Similar to China, with the exception of grave human rights violations, India prefers noninterventionism in the domestic affairs of other states. If and when intervention is carried out, India has supported a multilateral coalition versus unilateral actions by superpowers. The United States has preferred a unilateral course of action in international affairs for the past few decades; it has exercised force without the consent of the United Nations. The United States has also bullied smaller powers economically as well as politically.

While Russia and China are indeed dissatisfied states in the current global order, India is still in play for both the United States on one side and

---

3. C. Uday Bhaskar, "Russia-India-China Meeting Shows a Multipolar World Order Is Taking Shape," *South China Morning Post*, December 15, 2017, http://www.scmp.com/com ment/insight-opinion/article/2124329/russia-india-china-meeting-shows-multipolar-world -order

Russia and China on the other. Indeed, it has become the lynchpin in determining the future of the global system. In this chapter, we examine relations between India and China to determine whether or not India is indeed still in play and whether or not the United States can continue to maintain its global hegemonic status and thus the unipolar system, or if India has allied itself with Russia and China and truly supports change toward a multipolar system.

India-China Ties

The Indo-Chinese relationship can be understood as a geostrategic struggle with increasing commercial ties and cooperation (Malone 2011, 129). Both states are engaged in a struggle to dominate the Indian Ocean region as well as Central and East Asia. India and China have tried to improve bilateral ties that are at present largely hinged on economic cooperation. They have also worked to cooperate in multilateral institutions such as the talks to combat global climate change. Nevertheless, relations between the two countries undergo periods of "coolness" as their economies continue to grow rapidly. Moreover, India is increasingly being courted by the United States and other Western states as a counterbalance to China's strength and aggression (Malone 2011).

Historically, China has allied with Pakistan given their mutual interests vis-à-vis India. Through the Cold War, a global rivalry emerged involving the United States, Pakistan, and China on one side and India and the Soviet Union on the other. It is only recently that the United States has forged closer ties with India, given Pakistan's unreliable and lackluster performance as an ally. India's strong commitment to democracy, multilateral international institutions, and peaceful growth and development are appealing to the United States as a trustworthy partner in Asia. India and the United States also share a strong passion for countering rising extremism and global terrorism. Thus, snapshot images of the current global interactions suggest growing closeness between India and the United States and rising animosity and competition between the India and China. However, these snapshot images are devoid of historical context and provide an incomplete picture of the status of ties between India and China and India and the United States. For instance, "the bilateral interactions of the 1980s and the early 1990s created a foundation for future cooperation and institutionalization of efforts to find a permanent settlement to the border dispute" between India and China (Malone 2011, 138). The year 2006 was declared to be the India-

China friendship year and the two states engaged in a yearlong exchange of diplomatic personnel and cultural programs. China also overtook the United States as India's largest trading partner starting in 2013.

Recent Developments in the Relationship

In 2017, the Doklam incident, a 73-day military standoff over border disputes in the trilateral region between Bhutan, China, and India, took place. Since then a series of visits by high-level personnel including a meeting between Indian Prime Minister Narendra Modi and Chinese President Xi Jinping on the sidelines of the September 2017 BRICS summit in the Chinese city of Xiamen have taken place. A series of Track 1 meetings have been set up including a China-India strategic economic dialogue held in April 2018 as well as a likely visit by Chinese commerce minister Zhing Shanto to discuss WTO related issues. There has been a steady improvement of ties between India and China since the Doklam incident; both states are working to reduce tensions and return to normalcy.

India and China are increasingly seen as rivals vying for regional hegemony in the Asian sphere. Most conflict theories are based on the notion that two rising powers with rapidly growing economies and aspirations to become major global powers cannot coexist peacefully within Asia. India is suspicious of encirclement by China, or the "string of pearls" strategy that attempts to choke India by isolating it and cutting off connections to various trade routes—this is based upon China's attempts to create military and naval bases and control strategic ports such as Gwadar in Pakistan and Hambantota in Sri Lanka. China is wary of the Quad alliance of India, Japan, Australia, and the United States, which it considers to be an attempt to encircle China. India and China have differences over issues such as the China–Pakistan economic corridor and China's continuous blocking of efforts at the United Nations to declare Jaish-e-Mohammad leader Masood Azhar a global terrorist. In spite of these differences trade between the two countries increased by 18percent in 2017. After the Doklam incident there was a discussion on boycotting Chinese goods, and India imposed antidumping duties on 98 Chinese commodities.

There are several points of cooperation between the two states as well. A statement issued by the Indian Ministry of External Affairs after the visit of Indian foreign minister Vijay Gokhale to China in February 2018 suggested enhanced engagement between the two states. India recently supported China's bid for the vice presidency of the Financial Action Task Force, an international watchdog organization that seeks to combat money laundering and the financing of terrorism. In response, China supported the US bid to place Pakistan on the gray list for having engaged in terror sponsorship (as long accused by India). It is worth noting that the United States was interested in nominating Japan for the role of vice president of the organization. However, India's support was crucial in tilting the balance in favor of China. Evidence such as this lends support to our argument about India serving as the lynchpin in the systemic shift toward a multipolar global order.

Cooperation with China is very desirable for India for reasons outlined below. India believes that China can exert pressure on Pakistan to eliminate support of terrorist organizations such as LeT and JeM. China has considerable influence over Pakistan due to its economic investments in the country.[4] India is also looking to court Chinese investment in states such as Gujarat, West Bengal, and Maharashtra, among others. India and China share common ground on climate change and on international tariffs on trade. The 2019 move by President Trump to impose trade tariffs on imports of steel and aluminum and exhibit protectionism, thereby starting a global trade war, is unpopular with both India and China, whose economies are heavily dependent on exports. Both India and China want to make the 21st century the Asian century.

Several different arguments can be made with regard to the future relationships between India, China, and the United States. We use evidence-based arguments to project the future ties between these parties. India has attempted to delicately balance its newly emerging friendship with the United States along with its economic ties and dependence on China. India is also rapidly increasing its military expenditures and bolstering its naval presence in the Indian Ocean region to counterbalance China's assertive role. While it is generally expected that India will aid the United States in countering China's rise and aggression in Asia and beyond, we argue that Sino-Indian ties are actually far more institutionalized that Indo-American ties. As a result, we expect that while India will attempt to balance China, it will not adopt an aggressive posture vis-à-vis China.

Data and Analysis

In this chapter we analyze Indo-Chinese treaties from India's founding to 2019. India's freedom from the United Kingdom is the best point to begin

---

4. While Pakistan was also reliant on American foreign aid and the United States exerted pressure on Pakistan to not sponsor terrorism, it failed to have much impact.

the analysis, and ensures that all of the bilateral treaties that have been signed by India and China are included in the analysis. Similar to India, China had a change in its regime in 1949, meaning that it is a natural starting point to examine the relationship.

As mentioned previously, a Treaty A is considered to be nested under Treaty B if it explicitly makes a reference to the earlier treaty. A tie between two treaties is considered to be present when one explicitly references the other, that is, it is nested within the other. A relationship is considered to have institutionalized cooperation when the total number of ties in the relationship is equal to or greater than the total number of bilateral treaties between the two states. It is considered to have ad hoc cooperation when the total number of ties is less than the total number of bilateral treaties between the two states. Table 19 provides the cooperation levels between India and China and shows that while there is cooperation, it is not institutionalized cooperation, but rather ad hoc cooperation.

It is interesting to note that most of the bilateral treaties were signed in the last two decades of the analysis. This coincides with the rise of Chinese power in the region, and is evidence that India is at least attempting to cooperate with China instead of fully balancing against it. In contrast to the relationship between India and Japan, India is cautious with institutionalizing its cooperation with China. In other words, India is cooperating with both China and Japan, but has not fully aligned itself with either state.

More importantly, India and Russia have signed a total of 49 bilateral treaties between 1992 and 2015. India and China have signed a comparable 47 treaties in the same time period. However, India and the United States have signed a mere 9 treaties in the same time period. This data suggests that it is premature to jump to the conclusion that India is drifting from the Soviet sphere of influence and growing closer to the United States. It is also difficult to argue that India will ally with the United States to balance against the rise of China and potentially help to counter China's aggression in hot spots such as the South China Sea or its influence in Central and East Asia.

Network Analysis

While table 19 provides information on the levels of institutionalized cooperation over time, it does not provide information on which issue areas are significant to each dyad. To determine this, we use network analysis to study the patterns in these dyads. The more times a specific treaty is mentioned by other treaties, the more significant it becomes to the bilateral rela-

Table 19. Levels of Cooperation between India and China, 1954–2019

Year	Treaties	Ties	Cooperation Score
1950	0	0	0
1960	3	1	.333
1970	3	1	.333
1980	3	1	.333
1990	11	2	.182
2000	45	19	.475
2010	112	58	.518
2019	161	87	.540

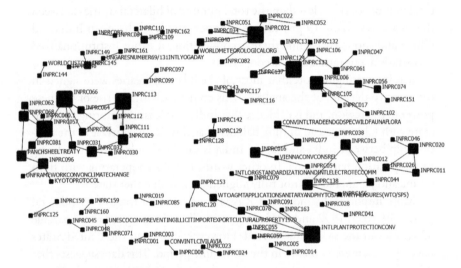

Fig. 15. Indo-China Treaty Network

tionship. The size of a treaty on the network map is representative of its significance to the bilateral relationship. The network map presents information on which treaties are connected to each other, as well as which treaties are central to the network; the degree centrality measure can help identify the lodestone treaties, which are the most central to the relationship. We present three different network maps: figure 15 presents the Indo-Chinese treaty network.

In figure 15, the Indo-Chinese treaty map, there are small pockets of institutionalized cooperation. There are a group of treaties that are cross-referenced by each other; India and China build upon Treaty 10 and Treaty 18—all security related treaties signed afterward explicitly reference these

Table 20. Lodestone Treaties in Sino-Indian Relationship

Treaty Number	Name	Number of Ties
INPRC133	MOU between India and China on Strengthening Cooperation on Trans Border Rivers	5.00
INPRC057	Declarations on Principles for Relations and Comprehensive Cooperation between India and China	5.00
INPRC113	Agreement between India and China on Establishment of a Working Mechanism for Consultation on Indo-China Border Affairs	5.00
INPRC021	Agreement of Science and Technology Cooperation between India and China (December 22, 1988)	5.00
IPPC	International Plant Protection Convention	5.00
INPRC066	Agreement between India and China on Political Parameters and Guiding Principles for the Settlement of India-China Boundary Question	5.00

lodestone treaties. In addition to this, there has been some attempt to build institutionalized cooperation on border trade. The network map suggests that India and China have signed several treaties on a wide range of issues including water sharing rights, intellectual property rights, border disputes, and trade and economic cooperation. However, they have not managed to link these divergent interests under the umbrella of one lodestone treaty. Although there is a lot of cooperation going on in this dyad, this cooperation has not been fully institutionalized. While Indo-Chinese cooperation is ad hoc, it does demonstrate a greater degree of cooperation than the Indo-American dyad. If we were to rank order these dyads in terms of their strength or levels of cooperation the Indo-Russian dyads would lead the way followed by the Indo-Chinese dyad, with a score of .540. The Indo-American dyad would come in last due to the lack of engagement between India and the United States with respect to bilateral treaties. Not only do they have a very small number of bilateral treaties, they also make no attempt to link new treaties to previous ones.

Table 20 shows a list of the lodestone treaties and their degree centrality scores, which indicates how central they are to the relationship. Based on this analysis, it is clear that India has a much more cooperative relationship with Russia than with India. While India and the US may continue to cooperate in the future, at present India remains firmly within the Russian sphere of influence. The United States should not count on India being willing to give up such a cooperative relationship with Russia to support the US over Russia. While India can continue to pursue cooperation with the United States on specific issues in an ad hoc manner, the data do not indicate that India's relationship with Russia will do anything but continue to grow stronger. India voted to abstain in a UN General Assembly vote to condemn Russia for invading Ukraine in 2022, further solidifying its ties to Russia.

Conclusion

The United States continues to spend much more on its military than most other countries combined. This hard power capability allows the US to continue to try to maintain its global hegemony and the unipolar system. However, as Nye (2003) correctly points out, hard power is not sufficient to maintain hegemony. The United States must work on its diplomacy and soft power to spread and maintain its global influence.

Both Russia and China have demonstrably argued against American hegemony, and have begun to actively challenge the United States. While neither Beijing nor Moscow is strong enough to challenge Washington alone, they have begun to form a bilateral alliance and to work together through multilateral institutions such as the Shanghai Cooperation Organization. However, even through bilateral and multilateral alliances, Beijing and Moscow can only challenge the United States directly within their own regions of power. For example, Moscow is currently challenging US hegemony in Ukraine, while Beijing challenges Washington in the South China Sea.

However, if the Sino-Russian alliance can begin to show the world an attractive alternative to the liberal global order, then the United States will begin to lose its hegemonic status. That is why India is the lynchpin to the global order. If India chooses to ally itself with Moscow and Beijing, then other countries will begin to follow suit and directly challenge US hegemony, thus leading to a multipolar system. However, if India allies itself with Washington, the Sino-Russian challenge will wither before it has had a chance to become a serious challenge to US hegemony.

The Sino-Indian relationship is not wholly cooperative. Yet Beijing and New Delhi have worked hard to improve their relations. Their relationship is close to being a cooperative one. Should China and India be able to overcome their differences and continue to cooperate, the Sino-Indian relationship should become just as strong as the Russo-Indian relationship. If the relationship does become stronger, then it will be at a cost to the US-Indian relationship, which will then lead to a very strong challenge to the liberal order.

Ultimately, we predict that the Sino-Indian relationship will continue to strengthen, and within the next couple of decades we shall see direct evidence of a direct challenge to US hegemony. The question that will be raised then is whether the US will be willing to peacefully accede to a multipolar system as Trump has seemed to suggest when pressed about the US commitment to defend Europe, or whether the US will use its hard power to preserve the unipolar system, in which case a global conflict could ensue.

9 • India's Place in the World Order

Revisionist or Status Quo Power?

The world order is currently undergoing a transition. It is directly under attack by revisionist powers such as China and Russia. Following the end of the Cold War, the United States was at the height of its hegemony. The bipolar system that had survived after World War II had given way to a new unipolar system with the US as the only superpower. The end of the Cold War saw euphoria and the idea that liberalism and the liberal order had truly triumphed. Politicians in the United States and Europe began to think of Russia as the vanquished enemy, and believed that there would no longer be any challenge to the liberal order.

The expansion of NATO into Eastern Europe and some of the former Soviet states began to alienate the Russians. While Russian president Boris Yeltsin tried to curry favor with the West, other politicians in Russia began to resent the fact that Russia was no longer treated as a great power and lamented the loss of power and prestige that accompanied the collapse of the Soviet Union. However, the collapse of the Soviet Union did leave Moscow in a very weak position and it was unable to convince Washington not to pursue NATO expansion or other initiatives that Moscow believed were not in its own interests.

Moscow's lack of power and influence allowed Washington to believe that it did not need to request advice from other great powers. In fact, US supremacy led to a sense that the US would act in its own interests and that other countries would follow the US lead because of its supremacy. After all, the United States spent more on its military than all of the other states combined.

In the early 1990s, Moscow's ally, Serbia, was embroiled in a civil war following the breakup of Yugoslavia. The Russians supported Serbia, whereas Washington supported the Bosnians. Russian volunteers went to Serbia to fight against the Bosnians in a perceived war in defense of Orthodox Christianity. The United States supported Bosnia, and later supported the Kosovar Muslims in their attempts to separate from Serbia.

Despite these issues, the Yeltsin administration still tried to cooperate with Washington and seek its support. In other words, it was more important for the Yeltsin administration to gain the support of the West than it was to adhere to its own strategic interests in the region. Yeltsin's actions alienated many policy makers in Russia, and stimulated resentment among Russians toward the West. Many politicians had been used to having a "seat at the table" and at least having their interests considered. During the Soviet era, they believed that the West feared Soviet power and thus did not take actions that would deliberately provoke Moscow. However, the Clinton administration's view of US supremacy made it very clear that Russia was to be considered a weak regional power and not a great power that had any right to help in the decision-making process in the global order.

Following September 11, 2001, the Bush administration further pursued a unilateral foreign policy. The administration adopted the Bush Doctrine, which stated that countries were either with the US or they were against the US. There was no place for consultation and negotiation. The US was going to take an American–centered approach to foreign policy and to protecting its interests. While the Russians initially saw the period following September 11 as a chance to cooperate with the United States and improve the relationship between the two countries, the Bush administration was not as interested in developing close ties and was hesitant to trust Russia. Further, Washington pursued such policies as withdrawing from the ABM Treaty and pursuing missile-defense systems in violation of many of the agreements of the Cold War era.

These actions by the Bush administration served to further enrage Russian policy makers and helped create a sense of nostalgia for the Soviet Union and a rise of Russian nationalism. The Russians felt as though they had once been a great power and that they were now being discounted. This really angered the Russians, and Russian president Putin used it to his great advantage. In fact, at the 2007 Munich security conference, Putin shocked the United States and the West by presenting a list of complaints about US hegemony and openly beginning to call for a specific shift to multilateralism from US unilateralism (Slobodchikoff 2017b).

By 2013, relations between the two countries became even more hostile. Ukraine became embroiled in a conflict between East and West over the West's spreading influence. The EU offered Ukraine a special cooperation agreement to form a relationship that would eventually lead to membership in the EU. Moscow was very apprehensive about this possible agreement and attempted to coerce Ukraine into not signing the agreement. They did this by offering to forgive debts incurred by Ukraine to Russia and by offering natural gas at extremely low prices. Brussels, on the other hand, offered the possibility of making it easier to access European markets for Ukrainian goods as well as many other benefits that the EU offered.

Ukrainian president Viktor Yanukovych was truly on the horns of a dilemma. The public in Kyiv and much of western Ukraine was very much in favor of signing the Association agreement with the EU. However, the southeastern part of Ukraine was Russian speaking and much more in favor of maintaining close ties with Russia. Yanukovych was faced with a zero-sum game. If he signed the Association agreement with the EU, he risked the access to gas that Ukraine had as well as alienating Moscow. If he chose not to sign the Association agreement, then Ukraine would have less debt and access to natural gas, but limited access to European markets or the wealth that eventual membership in the EU would bring. At first he said that he was going to sign the agreement, and then he decided against signing it.

When he announced that he was not going to sign the Association agreement, protests began in Kyiv against the president and his decision. These protests were aided by the West, and Western diplomats provided food and counsel to the protestors. While the Russians accused Washington of fomenting revolution in Ukraine, Washington argued that it was merely supporting peaceful protesters and aiding them in the exercise of freedom of speech.

The protests continued, mainly in Maidan Square in Kyiv, and eventually led to violence. Protesters were shot and the protests began to turn toward revolution. During this period Moscow again accused Washington of direct interference, but Washington denied these claims. What is clear is that Washington had developed a plan for a transition of government from Yanukovych to other leaders, such as Arseniy Yatsenyuk, who were deemed to be more palatable to the West.

Ultimately, the protests led to the escape of Yanukovych and a new government in Kyiv. The new government in Kyiv said that they would revisit the Black Sea Fleet treaties between Russia and Ukraine, and, in response, Russia sent in special forces to Crimea to maintain its military presence there. In a disputed referendum, Crimea voted to join the Russian Federation and secede from Ukraine. For the actions of Moscow, the United States and the EU imposed sanctions on Moscow and called for the immediate withdrawal of Russian troops and Crimea's return to Ukraine.

Following the events in Crimea, a rebellion started in the Donbas region of Ukraine. Washington accused Moscow of stoking the insurrection and providing military troops to aid in a battle of secession. Moscow denied this, and further sanctions were imposed by Washington on Moscow. The secession of the Donbas region led to a very violent civil war in which civilians were often targeted by both secessionist and government forces. Moscow recognized the right of the Donbas region to secede from Ukraine, but did not attempt to annex the Donbas the way it had annexed Crimea.

The fighting between Russia and the West over Ukraine led to a fissure between the two and a possible new cold war between Russia and the United States. The biggest difference between the Cold War era and the era right after the Ukrainian crisis was that ideology was not a major driving factor in the opposition. Rather, Moscow sought its opportunity to begin to challenge the liberal ideology and the global order developed by the United States. Moscow did not supply an immediate ideological choice between the liberal order and one proposed by Moscow. Instead, Moscow proposed an alternative to the liberal order, which was an order based on multilateralism.

Russia was not the only state that was dissatisfied with the liberal order. China had also become disenfranchised with the liberal order. While China viewed trade and economic cooperation as being very important, it also was very wary of any agreements that would lead to political changes or challenges to the regime in Beijing. Thus, Beijing was willing to loan money to, and actively seek economic cooperation with, both the United States and its allies in Europe, but it was very wary of any political entanglements.

Beijing had increasingly loaned money to the United States, and financed a lot of its debts. In 2008, Beijing had bought a fair amount of mortgages. Millions of people later defaulted on these mortgages, which led to the great recession of 2008. Even though Beijing did suffer some economically, its economy continued to grow. Its economy rivaled that of the United States, and it began to build up its military as well. Increasingly, it began to challenge the United States in the East Asian region, specifically in the South China Sea.

Economically, China began to challenge the United States by developing alternatives to the liberal institutions such as the International Monetary Fund and the World Bank. The Chinese alternatives were through the Shanghai Cooperation Organization as well as through BRICS (Brazil, Russia, India, China, and South Africa). One of those institutions, the East Asian Development Bank, was set up to be a direct competitor of the International Monetary Fund and the World Bank. The East Asian Development Bank loaned money to governments and rather than demand that democratic regime changes be made, it made no political requirements for receiving the funds. Instead, among the stipulations were that Chinese companies would have to work on the infrastructure projects and would be paid for them. If states were not able to repay their debts, then China would take over the infrastructure as a forfeit of collateral.

During this period of time, China developed the New Silk Road project. The idea behind this new project was to open up a new era of trade that would not be reliant upon the United States, but rather would allow increased trade between Beijing and many other parts of the world. This new project morphed into the One Belt One Road Initiative. Washington accused Beijing of using the One Belt One Road Initiative and the Confucius centers in Western Europe and the United States to challenge or begin to challenge the global liberal order.

The crisis in Ukraine served to increase cooperation between Russia and China. While they had started cooperating using the Shanghai Cooperation Organization, they still were often rivals in Central Asia and had even fought a border conflict prior to the collapse of the Soviet Union. However, as Russia's actions were met with sanctions from the West, Beijing refused to support those sanctions and officially took a neutral position on Russia's actions in the Crimea and Ukraine.

As Russia became more isolated, it sought to cooperate more with China, which was mutually beneficial. China began to invest more in the Russian economy, and the two countries began to work more closely militarily. Beijing saw this as an opportunity to gain a solid ally that was already opposed to the global liberal order. Moscow, on the other hand, saw more opportunities to open up the Chinese market to Russian goods as well as buy electronics and other consumer goods so that it did not have to rely on goods from the United States and the European Union. Further, Chinese power had grown enough that Russia was concerned with such a powerful neighbor so close to them, and by allying themselves with China they prevented a hostile neighbor.

When Donald Trump came to power in 2016, he further isolated China and began a trade war, using tariffs to try to stop the Chinese economy from becoming so powerful. These actions only further enhanced Sino-Russian cooperation and further allied the two powers. Both powers officially claimed their support for multilateralism and the end of the current global order. In other words, they identified themselves as revisionist powers interested in a shift from unipolarity and US primacy to multipolarity and a new global order that would be renegotiated with the great powers. Thus, the revisionist powers have established a stark choice for other states to follow. The revisionist powers are not strong enough yet to fully take on the liberal order. However, they do present an alternative to the liberal order, and if they can gain enough allies to challenge the world order, the order would have to change.

The current state of the world order is one that is under attack and it is unclear whether or not it can survive. To survive, it must maintain the goodwill and support of the great powers that accept the current world order. These are not only global great powers but also regional great powers. Following Lemke's hierarchical model of regional power, it is important that both global and regional powers support the global order or else the global order will fall.

Revisionist powers, on the other hand, must convince enough of those global and regional great powers to be willing to change the global order and move in a multipolar direction. In other words, these regional and global great powers become important lynchpins to either maintaining or changing the global order. India is just such a great power. While some scholars have argued about whether or not it is a regional great power or a global great power, India is in a position to serve as a kingmaker in determining the fate of the global order. In this book we have examined India's relationships with both status quo powers (the United States, the EU, the United Kingdom, France, Germany, and Japan) and the main revisionist powers (Russia and China). Using network analysis measures and measures of cooperative relationships developed by Slobodchikoff (2013, 2014), we are able to determine whether India is more supportive of the status quo or whether it is a revisionist power.

It should be noted that India has continually professed its neutrality while simultaneously claiming to want to better its relationship with the United States and Western Europe while at the same time also pursuing a relationship with Russia. While India has not withdrawn support for the current global order, it has also argued and pushed for changes that would alter the current global hierarchy as well as the structure and composition of multilateral institutions. While India's foreign policy remains officially neutral, we seek to examine the country's true leanings. In order to do so, we examine India's bilateral ties with other great powers—both status quo and revisionist.

In this chapter, we first provide the details of the analysis of India's bilateral ties by examining India's relationships with both status quo and revisionist states. Then we look at India's relationships with each of those groups separately to determine whether or not there is evidence to show that India is either a revisionist or a status quo power. Finally, we use the rubric that we developed earlier in the book to make a final determination on India's status in the global order and what this means for the future of the global order.

Table 21. Cooperation Scores between India and the Great Powers

Bilateral Relationship	Cooperation Score	Power Status in Global Order
India-France	1.18	Status Quo
India-Japan	1.1	Status Quo
India-Russia	1.09	*Revisionist*
India-EU	1.08	Status Quo
India-China	.54	*Revisionist*
India-UK	.53	Status Quo
India-US	.50	**Hegemon**
India-Germany	.41	Status Quo

As table 21 shows, India has a highly cooperative relationship with four out of the eight states. The relationship between India and the United States, the global hegemon, has a low cooperation score. In fact, the bottom three states are status quo states. In contrast, the top two states ranked by levels of cooperation score are also status quo states. The first is India's relationship with France, as they share many interests in science and technology, nuclear energy, and defense. Similarly, India has a very cooperative relationship with Japan. Indo-Japanese ties are cemented by the need to balance the rise of China in Asia. However, it is interesting to note that the relationship between China and India has a higher cooperation score than that between the United States and India.

Unfortunately, as shown in table 21, there is little indication as to whether India's foreign policy aligns itself more with the status quo powers or the revisionist powers. To delve deeper, we examine each bilateral relationship in depth. We first start with the status quo powers and then examine India's relationship with the revisionist powers.

Is India a Status Quo Power?

If India were a status quo power, we would expect that it would have insti-tutionalized cooperative relationships with many of the major powers sup-porting the status quo. Specifically, the most important state would be the United States, and we should see evidence of institutionalized cooperative relationships with other developed democracies such as the United King-dom, France, Germany, and Japan. However, we don't see evidence of insti-tutionalized cooperation between India and the United States. Neither do we find evidence of institutionalized cooperation between India and the United Kingdom nor India and Germany. As table 22 shows, India has

Table 22. Cooperation Scores for Status Quo Powers

Year	US	EU	UK	France	Germany	Japan
1950	.33	0	0	1	0	.25
1960	.50	0	.50	.25	.17	.27
1970	.25	0	.33	.14	.42	.27
1980	.19	.75	.33	.27	.28	.23
1990	.26	.80	.33	.44	.28	.23
2000	.36	.75	.25	.38	.30	.85
2010	.45	.87	.62	.55	.41	**1.10**
2019	.50	**1.08**	.53	**1.18**	.41	**1.10**

developed institutionalized cooperation with the EU (1.08), France (1.18), and Japan (1.10). India maintains only ad hoc cooperation with the United States (.50), the United Kingdom (.53), and Germany (.41).

Of the status quo powers, India has the highest level of cooperation with France with a cooperation score of 1.18. India also has a high level of cooperation with Japan with a measure of 1.08. It is interesting to note that India reached an institutionalized cooperative relationship with Japan earlier than it reached an institutionalized cooperative relationship with any of the other status quo powers. By 2010, India had institutionalized its cooperation with Japan, whereas India institutionalized its cooperation with France only in 2020. India's cooperation with the EU is also institutionalized with a measure of 1.08. It also took until 2020 to reach an institutionalized relationship with the EU.

Based on this analysis, India does not meet the criteria for a status quo power. In fact, we can determine that it is not a status quo power. However, it is not clear whether India is a revisionist power.

As table 23 shows, the Indo-Russian cooperation is institutionalized with a score of 1.09, while the Sino-Indian cooperation is not institutionalized with a score of .54. This is not enough to indicate that India is a revisionist power, but it certainly indicates India's close historical ties with a revisionist power, Russia. While India and China are strategic rivals, they also attempt to cooperate on several issues. The Indo-Chinese cooperation score is higher than the Indo-British and Indo-German cooperation scores. It is interesting to note that both table 22 and table 23 show that India institutionalized its cooperation with both Japan and Russia by 2010, but those were the only two countries in the analysis with which India developed a cooperative relationship by 2010. Japan is a regional actor and a status quo power, while Russia is a revisionist power. In other words, even when looking at the status quo

Table 23. Comparison of India's Relationship with
Revisionist Powers

Year	Russia	China
1950	0	0
1960	.6667	.333
1970	.4375	.333
1980	.5926	.333
1990	.6094	.182
2000	.654	.475
2010	**1.074**	.518
2019	**1.09**	.540

and revisionist powers individually, India appears to have developed a self-interested foreign policy without regard to the global order. To further investigate whether or not India is a status quo or revisionist state, we now turn to the rubric developed earlier in the book to classify India's status in the global order.

Table 24 shows the rubric that would enable a categorization of India as either a status quo or a revisionist power. It has five possible categories: solid status quo power; leans status quo; neutral; leans revisionist; and solid revisionist power. We will go through each of the categories to determine which category best fits India's status in the global order.

To qualify as a solid status quo power, table 24 indicates that India should have an institutionalized cooperative relationship with each of the status quo great powers (see table 24). We find that this is not the case. While India has an institutionalized cooperative relationship with France, the EU, and Japan, it does not have an institutionalized cooperative relationship with the most important state in the status quo powers, which is the United States, nor does it have an institutionalized cooperative relationship with Germany or the United Kingdom. Thus, it is safe to argue that based on our methodology India cannot be classified as a solid status quo power.

To be classified as a power that leans status quo, India must have institutionalized cooperation with the United States, and develop ad hoc cooperation with the other major powers that are status quo. India does not have an institutionalized cooperative relationship with the United States, but it does have an institutionalized cooperative relationship with the EU, France, and Japan. This would certainly lead us to state that India might lean status quo. However, with the exception of Germany, India's relationship with the United States is one of the least institutionalized of all of the relationships examined in this book. Therefore, we determine that India does not lean status quo.

Table 24. Categorization of Status Quo vs. Revisionist Power

Solid Status Quo	Leans Status Quo	Undecided	Leans Revisionist	Solid Revisionist
Institutionalized Cooperative Relationship with US	Institutionalized Cooperative Relationship with US	Either no institutionalized cooperative relationships **OR** Institutionalized Cooperative Relationship with Russia (Revisionist) and the United States (Status Quo).	Institutionalized Cooperative Relationship with Russia	Institutionalized Cooperative Relationship with Russia
Institutionalized Cooperative Relationship with UK	Ad hoc or Institutionalized Relationship with EU		Ad hoc or Institutionalized Relationship with China	Institutionalized Cooperative Relationship with China
Institutionalized Cooperative Relationship with France	Ad hoc or Institutionalized Relationship with France _or_ Germany		Lacks Institutionalized Cooperative Relationship with US	
Institutionalized Cooperative Relationship with Germany	Ad hoc or Institutionalized Relationship with Japan			
Institutionalized Cooperative Relationship with EU				
Institutionalized Cooperative Relationship with Japan				
Lacks Institutionalized Cooperative Relationship with Russia				

To be classified as an undecided or neutral power, we would have to demonstrate that India maintains cooperative relationships with all of the great powers regardless of whether they are status quo or revisionist, or that they don't have an institutionalized cooperative relationship with any of the great powers. This category is important because India claims neutrality in its foreign policy. India has not entirely jettisoned its nonaligned historical approach and continues to pursue a nonaligned foreign policy. However, there is evidence that India is not undecided according to the definition and classification provided. It does not have an institutionalized cooperative relationship with the United States (the main status quo power), but does have an institutionalized cooperative relationship with Russia, which is a revisionist state.

Table 24 also indicates that to be classified as a solid revisionist power, India would have to have institutionalized cooperative relationships with both China and Russia. India does have an institutionalized cooperative relationship with Russia, but not with China. India's cooperation score with China is .54, which is better than its cooperation score with the United States, but it is not an institutionalized cooperative relationship. As a result, Indo-Chinese cooperation can be termed ad hoc. Further, it is important to note that the cooperation score is higher for India's relationship with China than it is for India's relationship with the United States. The score does not qualify this bilateral relationship as institutionalized cooperation. However, given that the cooperation score between India and China is higher than that between India and the United States, India has a better relationship with China (a country that it has had conflictual relations with in the past) than with the United States (the leading status quo power). Based on our methodology, India is classified as a state that leans revisionist.

That is not to say that India has turned its back on the global order, merely that it leans more revisionist than status quo at this time. In other words, India is still in play for both the status quo and revisionist powers. Both China and the United States need to work on their relationships with India to convince India to side with them in the current challenge to the global order. This is especially true for the United States, as Washington has one of the lowest levels of cooperation with India (0.5). It is only slightly lower than the Indo-Chinese cooperation score, but given the India-China rivalry, one would expect that if India were more interested in being a status quo power then its cooperation score with the US would be higher than that with China.

Ultimately, there is still much diplomacy that needs to take place. Despite the rhetoric of the United States turning and pivoting to Asia, the data show that this has not happened. If the United States wants to maintain its position as the global hegemon and maintain the current world order then it has a lot of work to do to gain the trust of New Delhi and really begin to institutionalize a cooperative relationship. At this point, the United States cannot count on India's support in a competition for the world order, but it also cannot completely discount India's support in the future. Similarly, while China has attempted to improve its relationship with India, it still has a lot of work ahead if it wants to convince India to join a challenge to the global order. India seems much more inclined to support multilateralism, but yet is still concerned about Chinese dominance in the region. It is also concerned that if China were to gain dominance, we would not see multipolarity, but would witness either a new bipolar system where the US and China would be the dominant powers, or, if the challenge to the global order is successful, possibly even a unipolar system where China would take the place of the United States as global hegemon.

The global order is currently at an inflection point and the battle to maintain it is underway. There is no guarantee of a shift in the global order nor is there a guarantee that the current global order will remain. There are many challenges to the current global order and those challenges are both internal and external. We have seen a rise of nationalism internally in the United States and within its allies that has shaken the stability of the global order. The rift between Russia and the United States as well as the rift between the United States and China have further created cleavages between those powers. One thing is absolutely clear, and that is that India will play a prominent part in deciding what the new global order will look like. That is not to say that India will be the only state that will have significant input in determining the next global order, merely that it will be one of the most important states that will have significant input in determining the next global order. The next decade of the 21st century will be decisive in determining whether or not the current global order can survive. This study should be expanded to other regional great powers in different regions of the world to determine their status in the global order. At that point it would be possible to make a determination of the likelihood of survival for the current global order.

While the global order's two strongest powers, the United States and China, are currently locked in a battle to determine the next global order, India continues to become stronger. It is not inconceivable that within the next century India could become one of the most powerful states in the system. However, currently India is not vying for control of the global order. Instead, it is content with holding an important seat at the table of powerful states and its status as kingmaker for the next hegemon who will create the new global order.

References

Abbott, Kenneth W., Robert O. Keohane, Andrew Moravcsik, Anne-Marie Slaughter, and Duncan Snidal. 2000. "The Concept of Legalization." *International Organization* 54 (3): 401–19.

Acharya, Amitav. 2007. "The Emerging Regional Architecture of World Politics." *World Politics* 59 (4): 629–52.

Aggarwal, Vinod K. 1998. *Institutional Designs for a Complex World: Bargaining, Linkages, and Nesting.* Ithaca: Cornell University Press.

Agreement between India and Japan for Cooperation in the Peaceful Uses of Nuclear Energy. 2016. India Bilateral Treaties and Agreements. November 11. Retrieved from Ministry of External Affairs, India: https://mea.gov.in/TreatyList.htm?1

Agreement between India and United States of America on Cooperation on a Joint Clean Energy Research and Development Centre. 2010. India Bilateral Treaties and Agreements. November 4. Retrieved from Ministry of External Affairs, India: https://mea.gov.in/TreatyList.htm?1

Agreement for Cooperation in Earth Sciences between India and United States of America Framework Agreement between India and United States of America for Cooperation in the Exploration and Use of Outer Space for Peaceful Purposes. 2008. India Bilateral Treaties and Agreements. February 1. Retrieved from Ministry of External Affairs India: https://mea.gov.in/TreatyList.htm?1

Agreement on Science and Technology Cooperation between India and United States of America. 2005. India Bilateral Treaties and Agreements. October 17. Retrieved from Ministry of External Affairs India: https://mea.gov.in/TreatyList.htm?1

Ambrosio, Thomas. 2017. "The Architecture of Alignment: The Russia–China Relationship and International Agreements." *Europe-Asia Studies* 69 (1): 110–56.

Ambrosio, Thomas, and William A. Lange. 2016. "The Architecture of Annexation? Russia's Bilateral Agreements with South Ossetia and Abkhazia." *Nationalities Papers* 44 (5): 673–93.

Amended MOU between the Department of Space and the Department of Science and Technology of the Government of the Republic of India and the National Aeronautics and Space Administration and the National Oceanic and Atmospheric Administration of the USA for Scientific Cooperation in the Areas of Earth and Atmospheric

Sciences. 2012. India Bilateral Treaties and Agreements. December 17. Retrieved from Ministry of External Affairs India: https://mea.gov.in/TreatyList.htm?1

Ayers, Alyssa. 2018. "The U.S. Indo-Pacific Strategy Needs More Indian Ocean." Expert Brief, Council on Foreign Relations, May 25 (updated January 22, 2019). https://www.cfr.org/expert-brief/us-indo-pacific-strategy-needs-more-indian-ocean

Bakshi, Jyotsna. 2006. "India-Russia Defence Co-Operation." *Strategic Analysis* 30 (2): 449–66.

Banerji, Arun Kumar. 1977. *India and Britain, 1947–68: The Evolution of Post-colonial Relations*. Calcutta: Minerva Associates. https://catalogue.nla.gov.au/Record/2553505

Baruah, Darshana. 2016. "Toward Strategic Economic Cooperation between India and Japan." Carnegie India. https://carnegieendowment.org/files/Darshana_Baruah_India_and_Japan.pdf

Basrur, Rajesh. 2011. "India: A Major Power in the Making." In *Major Powers and the Quest for Status in International Politics: Global and Regional Perspectives*, edited by Thomas J. Volgy, Renato Corbetta, Keith A. Grant, and Ryan G. Baird, 181–202. New York: Palgrave.

Basu, Titli. 2014. "India-Japan Relations: An Enduring Partnership." *Indian Foreign Affairs Journal* 9 (3): 266.

Bhattacharya, Purusottam. 1996. "India and Germany: Challenges for a Partnership in Development." *International Studies* 33 (2): 183–203.

Bialer, Seweryn. 1982. *Stalin's Successors: Leadership, Stability and Change in the Soviet Union*. Cambridge: Cambridge University Press.

Boulding, Kenneth. 1962. *Conflict and Defense*. New York: Harper and Brothers.

Brewster, David. 2010. "The India-Japan Security Relationship: An Enduring Security Partnership?" *Asian Security* 6 (2): 95–120.

Budhwar, Prem K. 2007. "India-Russia Relations: Past, Present and the Future." *India Quarterly* 63 (3): 51–83.

Bueno de Mesquita, Bruce. 1981. "Risk, Power Distributions, and the Likelihood of War." *International Studies Quarterly* 25 (4): 541–68.

Bull, Hedley. 2012. *The Anarchical Society: A Study of Order in World Politics*. New York: Macmillan International Higher Education.

Carter, Barry E., Phillip R. Trimble, and Allen S. Weiner. 2007. *International Law*. New York: Aspen Publishers.

Chacko, Priya. 2014. "A New 'Special Relationship'? Power Transitions, Ontological Security, and India–US Relations." *International Studies Perspectives* 15 (3): 329–46.

Chadha, Astha. 2020. "India's Foreign Policy towards Japan: Special Partnership amid Regional Transformation." *Ritsumeikan Journal of Asia Pacific Studies* 38 (1): 19–37.

Chengappa, Raj. 2000. "Indo-Japanese Relations: PM Yoshiro Mori's Visit Holds Promise of Return to Normalcy." *India Today*, August 28. https://www.indiatoday.in/magazine/diplomacy/story/20000828-indo-japanese-relations-pm-yoshiro-moris-visit-holds-promise-of-return-to-normalcy-777913-2000-08-28

Churchill, Winston. 2009. *Iron Curtain Speech*. Toledo, OH: Great Neck Publishers.

Commission on Security and Cooperation in Europe. 2006. *The Shanghai Cooperation*

Organization: Is It Undermining U.S. Interests in Central Asia? September 26. Washington, DC: CSCE.

Convention on International Liability for Damage Caused by Space Objects.

Convention on Narcotic Drugs.

Convention on Psychotropic Substances.

Cooley, Alexander. 2012. *Great Games, Local Rules: The New Power Contest in Central Asia.* Oxford: Oxford University Press.

Davis, Christina L. 2004. "International Institutions and Issue Linkage: Building Support for Agricultural Trade Liberalization." *American Political Science Review* 98 (1): 153–69.

Dhaka, Ambrish. 2009. "The Geopolitics of Energy Security and the Response to Its Challenges by India and Germany." *Geopolitics* 14 (2): 278–99.

DiCicco, Jonathan M., and Jack S. Levy. 1999. "Power Shifts and Problem Shifts: The Evolution of the Power Transition Research Program." *Journal of Conflict Resolution* 43 (6): 675–704.

Dipanjan, Roy Choudhary. 2019. "Narendra Modi: Russia Awards PM Narendra Modi with Highest State Honour." *Economic Times*, April 12. https://economictimes.indiatimes.com/news/politics-and-nation/russian-award-for-pm-narendra-modi/articleshow/68848666.cms

Downs, George W., David M. Rocke, and Peter N. Barsoom. 1996. "Is the Good News about Compliance Good News about Cooperation?" *International Organization* 50 (3): 379–406.

Eliott, John. 2017. "India Considers a Leading Role in De-Centralised British Commonwealth." *Wire*, November 29. https://thewire.in/external-affairs/india-considers-leading-role-de-centralised-british-commonwealth

Everett, Martin G., and Stephen P. Borgatti. 1999. "The Centrality of Groups and Classes." *Journal of Mathematical Sociology* 23 (3): 181–201.

Farley, M. S. 1939. "India and Japan Seek to Reach New Agreement." *Far Eastern Survey*, 289–90.

Ganguly, Sumit. 2003. "The Start of a Beautiful Friendship? The United States and India." *World Policy Journal* 20 (1): 25–30.

Ganguly, Sumit, and Andrew Scobell. 2005. "India and the United States: Forging a Security Partnership?" *World Policy Journal* 22 (2): 37–44.

Ghosh, Madhuchanda. 2008. "India and Japan's Growing Synergy: From a Political to a Strategic Focus." *Asian Survey* 48 (2): 282–302.

Gibbs, Joseph. 1999. *Gorbachev's Glasnost: The Soviet Media in the First Phase of Perestroika.* College Station: Texas A&M University Press.

Gilpin, Robert. 1981. *War and Change in World Politics.* Cambridge: Cambridge University Press.

Goddeeris, Idesbald. 2011. "EU-India Relations." *Policy Brief 16*, 7. Leuven, Belgium: Leuven Centre for Global Governance Studies.

Goldstein, Judith. 1996. "International Law and Domestic Institutions: Reconciling North American 'Unfair' Trade Laws." *International Organization* 50 (4): 541–64.

Goldstein, Judith, and Joanne Gowa. 2002. "US National Power and the Post-war Trading Regime." *World Trade Review* 1 (2): 153–70.

Goldstein, Judith, Miles Kahler, Robert O. Keohane, and Anne-Marie Slaughter. 2000.

"Introduction: Legalization and World Politics." *International Organization* 54 (3): 385–99.

Gorbachev, Mikhail. 1987a. *Perestroika: New Thinking for Our Country and the World.* New York: Harper and Row.

Gorbachev, Mikhail. S. 1987b. *Toward a Better World.* New York: Vintage.

Goyal, Tanu M., Ramneet Goswami, and Tincy Sara Solomon. 2014. *Facilitating Bilateral Investments between India and Germany: The Role of Negotiations and Reforms.* Working Paper No. 282. Indian Council for Research on International Economic Relations. https://icrier.org/pdf/working_paper_282.pdf

Grieco, Joseph, Robert Powell, and Duncan Snidal. 1993. "The Relative-Gains Problem for International Cooperation." *American Political Science Review* 87 (3): 729–43.

Gusman, Mikhail. 2015. "Indian PM Narendra Modi: Russia Remains Our Principal Partner." *Tass,* December 22. http://tass.ru/en/world/846052

Hayden, Michael. 2018. "Global Security." Lecture to the Alabama World Affairs Council, April 11, Montgomery, AL.

Henisz, Witold J., and Edward D. Mansfield. 2006. "Votes and Vetoes: The Political Determinants of Commercial Openness." *International Studies Quarterly* 50 (1): 189–211. https://repository.upenn.edu/mgmt_papers/33/

Huntington, Samuel P. [1968] 2006. *Political Order in Changing Societies.* New Haven: Yale University Press.

Ikenberry, G. John. 2011. "Crisis of the Old Order." In *Liberal Leviathan: The Origins, Crisis, and Transformation of the American World Order,* 1–32. Princeton: Princeton University Press.

India and Japan Vision 2025 Special Strategic and Global Partnership Working Together for Peace and Prosperity of the Indo Pacific Region and the World. 2015. India Bilateral Treaties and Agreements. December 12. Retrieved from Ministry of External Affairs India: https://mea.gov.in/TreatyList.htm?1

India Today. 2015. "Swadeshi Movement: Timeline and Important Facts That You Must Know." *India Today,* August 7. https://www.indiatoday.in/education-today/gk-curr ent-affairs/story/swadeshi-movement-286966-2015-08-07

"India, UK Putting in Place Building Blocks for Trade Pact, Says UK High Commissioner." 2020. *Hindu Business Line,* January 30. https://www.thehindubusinessline.com /news/world/india-uk-putting-in-place-building-blocks-for-trade-pact-says-uk-hi gh-commissioner/article30694644.ece

Jaffrelot, Christophe. 2006. *India and the European Union: the Charade of a Strategic Partnership.* https://hal-sciencespo.archives-ouvertes.fr/hal-01065630/document

Jain, Rajendra K., and Shreya Pandey. 2019. "The EU Global Strategy and EU–India Relations: A Perceptions Study." In *Shaping the EU Global Strategy,* edited by Natalia Chaban and Martin Holland, 101–26. Cham, Switzerland: Palgrave Macmillan.

Joint Declaration between India and Japan on the Conclusion of the Comprehensive Economic Partnership Agreement, India-Japan. 2010. India Bilateral Treaties and Agreements. October 25. Retrieved from Ministry of External Affairs India: https:// mea.gov.in/TreatyList.htm?1

Joint Statement between India and Japan on the Occasion of the Fourth Meeting of the Japan India Energy Dialogue. 2010. India Bilateral Treaties and Agreements. April 30. Retrieved from Ministry of External Affairs India: https://mea.gov.in/TreatyList .htm?1

Joint Statement by Prime Minister Dr. Manmohan Singh and Prime Minister Dr. Yukio Hatoyama on New Stage of India-Japan Strategic and Global Partnership. 2009. India Bilateral Treaties and Agreements. December 29. Retrieved from Ministry of External Affairs India: https://mea.gov.in/TreatyList.htm?1

Joint Statement on Cooperation in Energy and Environment between India and United States of America. 2000. India Bilateral Treaties and Agreements. March 22. Retrieved from Ministry of External Affairs India: https://mea.gov.in/TreatyList .htm?1

Joint Statement on the Advancement of the Strategic and Global Partnership between India and Japan. 2008. India Bilateral Treaties and Agreements. October 22. Retrieved from Ministry of External Affairs India: https://mea.gov.in/TreatyList .htm?1

Joshi, Nirmala. 2007. "India-Russia Relations and the Strategic Environment in Eurasia." In *Eager Eyes Fixed on Eurasia, Russia and Its Neighbors in Crisis*, edited by Iwashita Akihiro, 196–210. Hokkaido: Slavic Research Centre, Hokkaido University, Sapporo.

Kalavalapalli, Yogendra, Amrit Raj, and Gouri Shah. 2014. "How Maruti Changed the Dynamics of Indian Car Industry." *Live Mint*, February 13. https://www.livemint.com /Companies/js6mNCIQXBVo5tnBnspzVI/How-Maruti-800-changed-the-dynam ics-of-Indian-car-industry.html

Kapur, S. Paul, and Sumit Ganguly. 2007. "The Transformation of US-India Relations: An Explanation for the Rapprochement and Prospects for the Future." *Asian Survey* 47 (4): 642–56.

Kaura, Vinay. 2019. "Deepening Relationship between Russia and China: Implications for India in an Era of Strategic Uncertainty." *Indian Journal of Asian Affairs* 32 (1/2): 49–66.

Kelley, Judith. 2007. "Who Keeps International Commitments and Why? The International Criminal Court and Bilateral Nonsurrender Agreements." *American Political Science Review* 101 (3): 573–89.

Kennan, George. 1991. "The Long Telegram" (1946). In *Origins of the Cold War: The Novikov, Kennan, and Roberts "Long Telegrams" of 1946*, edited by Kenneth M. Jensen, 19–31. Washington, DC: United States Institute of Peace.

Keohane, Robert. O. 2005. *After Hegemony: Cooperation and Discord in the World Political Economy*. Princeton: Princeton University Press.

Keohane, Robert. O., and Lisa L. Martin. 1995. "The Promise of Institutionalist Theory." *International Security* 20 (1): 39–51.

Khashimwo, Pamreihor. 2015. "India and Germany: Global Partnership in 21st Century." *International Journal of Scientific Research and Management* 3 (6): 3188–95.

Koremenos, Barbara. 2002. "Can Cooperation Survive Changes in Bargaining Power? The Case of Coffee." *Journal of Legal Studies* 31 (s1): S259–83.

Koremenos, Barbara. 2005. "Contracting around International Uncertainty." *American Political Science Review* 99 (4): 549–65.

Koremenos, Barbara. 2009. *International Institutions as Solutions to Underlying Games of Cooperation*. IBEI Working Papers. Barcelona: Institut Barcelona d'Estudis Internacionals.

Koremenos, Barbara, Charles Lipson, and Duncan Snidal. 2001. "The Rational Design of International Institutions." *International Organization* 55 (4): 761–99.

Korhonen, Keijo. 2010. Former Foreign Minister of Finland, personal interview by Michael O. Slobodchikoff. Tucson, AZ.

Kronstadt, K. Alan. 2005. "US-India Bilateral Agreements in 2005." With Foreign Affairs, Defense, and Trade Division. Washington, DC: Congressional Information Service, Library of Congress.

Kumar, Sumit. 2016. "New Momentum for India-Russia Relations?" *The Diplomat*, January 3. http://thediplomat.com/2016/01/new-momentum-for-india-russia-relations/

Kundu, Nivedita Das. 2008. "India's Strategic Cooperation with Russia and Its 'Near Abroad' States." *India Quarterly* 64 (4): 73–101.

Kydd, Andrew. 2000. "Trust, Reassurance, and Cooperation." *International Organization* 54 (2): 325–57.

Kydd, Andrew. 2001. "Trust Building, Trust Breaking: The Dilemma of NATO Enlargement." *International Organization* 55 (4): 801–28.

Latora, V., and M. Marchiori. 2007. "A Measure of Centrality Based on Network Efficiency." *New Journal of Physics* 9 (6): 188.

Leeds, Brett Ashley, and Burcu Savun. 2007. "Terminating Alliances: Why Do States Abrogate Agreements?" *Journal of Politics* 69 (4): 1118–32.

Lemke, Douglas. 2002. *Regions of War and Peace*. Cambridge: Cambridge University Press.

Lynch, Thomas F. 2017. "The Phases of Growth: India-Japan Strategic Partnership in the 21st Century." *South Asia Journal*, September 16. http://southasiajournal.net/the-phases-of-growth-india-japan-strategic-partnership-in-the-21st-century/

Malone, David M. 2011. *Does the Elephant Dance? Contemporary Indian Foreign Policy*. Oxford: Oxford University Press.

Martin, Michael F., and K. Alan Kronstadt. 2007. "India-US Economic and Trade Relations." Washington, DC: Congressional Research Service, Library of Congress.

Mathur, Arpita. 2012. *India-Japan Relations: Drivers, Trends and Prospects*. Singapore: S. Rajaratnam School of International Studies.

Matlock, Jack F. 2004. *Reagan and Gorbachev: How the Cold War Ended*. New York: Random House.

Mattli, Walter, and Tim Büthe. 2003. "Setting International Standards: Technological Rationality or Primacy of Power?" *World Politics* 56 (1): 1–42.

McNair, Brian. 2006. *Glasnost, Perestroika and the Soviet Media*. New York: Routledge.

Mearsheimer, John J. 2001. *The Tragedy of Great Power Politics*. New York: W. W. Norton.

Milner, Helen V. 1999. "The Political Economy of International Trade." *Annual Review of Political Science* 2 (1): 91–114.

Ministry of Foreign Affairs Japan. 2018. "India–Japan Relations." December. Retrieved from Ministry of Foreign Affairs Japan: https://mea.gov.in/Portal/ForeignRelation/Bilateral_brief_India-Japan_december_2018.pdf

Mohan, C. R., and Darshana M. Baruah. 2018. "Deepening the India-France Maritime Partnership." Carnegie India. https://carnegieindia.org/2018/02/23/deepening-india-france-maritime-partnership-pub-75630

Moravcsik, Andrew. 1997. "Taking Preferences Seriously: A Liberal Theory of International Politics." *International Organization* 51 (4): 513–53.

MOU between India and United States of America on Cooperative Measures to Increase

Awareness of and Support for Efforts to Combat Production, Distribution and Use of Illegal Drugs. 1994. India Bilateral Treaties and Agreements. May 18. Retrieved from Ministry of External Affairs India: https://mea.gov.in/TreatyList.htm?1

MOU between the Department of Space and the Department of Science and Technology of the Government of the Republic of India and the National Aeronautics and Space Administration and the National Oceanic and Atmospheric Administration of the USA for Scientific Cooperation in the Areas of Earth and Atmospheric Sciences. 1997. India Bilateral Treaties and Agreements. December 12. Retrieved from Ministry of External Affairs India: https://mea.gov.in/TreatyList.htm?1

MOU on Agriculture Cooperation and Food Security between India and United States of America. 2010. India Bilateral Treaties and Agreements. March 16. Retrieved from Ministry of External Affairs India: https://mea.gov.in/TreatyList.htm?1

Mukherjee, Rohan. 2018. "Japan's Strategic Outreach to India and the Prospects of a Japan–India Alliance." *International Affairs* 94 (4): 835–59.

Mutual Cooperation Agreement between India and United States of America for Reducing Demand, Preventing Illicit Use of Traffic in Drugs and for Matters Relating to Licit Trade in Opiates, Etc. 1990. India Bilateral Treaties and Agreements. March 29. Retrieved from Ministry of External Affairs India: https://mea.gov.in/TreatyList.htm?1

Narayanan, M. K. 2016. *India-Japan Relations in a Changing Asia*. Resource Paper 4, 1–18. Chennai, India: Indo-Japan Chamber of Commerce and Industry.

Nayar, Baldev Raj, and T. V. Paul. 2003. *India in the World Order: Searching for Major-Power Status*. Cambridge: Cambridge University Press.

Nye, Joseph S. 2003. *The Paradox of American Power: Why the World's Only Superpower Can't Go It Alone*. New York: Oxford University Press.

Ogden, Chris. 2014. *Indian Foreign Policy*. New York: John Wiley & Sons.

Onishi, Norimitsu. 2007. "Decades after War Trials, Japan Still Honors a Dissenting Judge." *New York Times*, August 7. https://www.nytimes.com/2007/08/31/world/asia/31memo.html

Opsahl, Tore, Filip Agneessens, and John Skvoretz. 2010. "Node Centrality in Weighted Networks: Generalizing Degree and Shortest Paths." *Social Networks* 32 (3): 245–51.

Organski, A. F. K. 1958. *World Politics*. New York: Knopf.

Organski, A. F. K., and Jacek Kugler. 1981. *The War Ledger*. Chicago: University of Chicago Press.

Panda, Aankit. 2018. "India, Japan Conclude First Dharma Guardian Military Exercise." *Diplomat*, November 15. https://thediplomat.com/2018/11/india-japan-conclude-first-dharma-guardian-military-exercise/

Panda, Rajaram. 2012. "India-Japan Defence Partnership." *Indian Foreign Affairs Journal* 7 (3): 311.

Panda, Rajaram. 2014. "India-Japan Relations: Dawn of a New Relationship?" *Indian Foreign Affairs Journal* 9 (2): 182.

Pardesi, Manjeet S. 2015. "Is India a Great Power? Understanding Great Power Status in Contemporary International Relations." *Asian Security* 11 (1): 1–30.

Paul, Joshy M. 2012. "India–Japan Security Cooperation: A New Era of Partnership in Asia." *Journal of the National Maritime Foundation of India* 8 (1): 31–50.

Poast, Paul. 2012. "Does Issue Linkage Work? Evidence from European Alliance Negotiations, 1860 to 1945." *International Organization* 66 (2): 277–310.

Putnam, Robert D. 1988. "Diplomacy and Domestic Politics: The Logic of Two-Level Games." *International Organization* 42 (3): 427–60.

Rajagopalan, R. 2020. "Evasive Balancing: India's Unviable Indo-Pacific Strategy." *International Affairs* 96 (1): 5–93. https://doi.org/10.1093/ia/iiz224

Rhamey, J. Patrick, Michael O. Slobodchikoff, and Thomas J. Volgy. 2015. "Order and Disorder across Geopolitical Space: The Effect of Declining Dominance on Interstate Conflict." *Journal of International Relations and Development* 18 (4): 383–406.

Rothermund, Dietmar. 2010. "Indo-German Relations: From Cautious Beginning to Robust Partnership." *India Quarterly* 66 (1): 1–12.

"Russia, India to Sell Jointly Manufactured Ka-226T Choppers Internationally." 2016. *Sputnik News*, January 29. http://sputniknews.com/business/20160129/10338946 31/ka-226t-helicopters-russia-india.html#ixzz3ycp0wNUv

Sarotte, Mary Elise. 2010. "Not One Inch Eastward? Bush, Baker, Kohl, Genscher, Gorbachev, and the Origin of Russian Resentment toward NATO Enlargement in February 1990." *Diplomatic History* 34 (1): 119–40.

Sinclair, Ian McTaggart. 1984. *The Vienna Convention on the Law of Treaties*. Manchester: Manchester University Press.

Slobodchikoff, Michael O. 2013. *Strategic Cooperation: Overcoming the Barriers of Global Anarchy*. Lanham, MD: Lexington Books.

Slobodchikoff, Michael O. 2014. *Building Hegemonic Order Russia's Way: Order, Stability, and Predictability in the Post-Soviet Space*. Lanham, MD: Lexington Books.

Slobodchikoff, Michael O. 2017a. "Strong as Silk: Changing Regional Alliances for China and the West." In *Changing Regional Alliances for China and the West*, edited by David Lane and Guichang Zhu. Lanham, MD: Lexington Books.

Slobodchikoff, Michael O. 2017b. "Challenging US Hegemony: The Ukrainian Crisis and Russian Regional Order." *Soviet and Post-Soviet Review* 44 (1): 76–95.

Slobodchikoff, Michael O., and Michael E. Aleprete. 2020. "The Impact of Russian-Led Eurasian Integration on the International Relations of the Post-Soviet Space." *Europe-Asia Studies* 73 (2): 1–15.

Slobodchikoff, Michael O., and Aakriti Tandon. 2017. "Shifting Alliances and Balance of Power in Asia: Transitions in the Indo-Russian Security Ties." *Asian Journal of Political Science* 25 (2): 159–75.

Slobodchikoff, Michael O., and Aakriti A. Tandon. 2019. "Cooperative Rivalry: Understanding Indo-Pakistani Ties Using Treaty Networks." *Journal of Indo-Pacific Affairs* 2 (3): 85–103.

Snidal, Duncan. 1991. "Relative Gains and the Pattern of International Cooperation." *American Political Science Review* 85 (3): 701–26.

Stewart-Ingersoll, Robert, and Derrick Frazier. 2012. *Regional Powers and Security Orders: A Theoretical Framework*. New York: Routledge.

Stolte, Carolien, and Harald Fischer-Tiné. 2012. "Imagining Asia in India: Nationalism and Internationalism (ca. 1905–1940)." *Comparative Studies in Society and History* 54 (1): 65–92.

Tandon, A. Aakriti, and Michael O. Slobodchikoff. 2019. "Building Trust: Cooperation between Rivals India and Pakistan." *Round Table* 108 (2): 189–201.

UN Framework Convention on Climate Change and Its Kyoto Protocol.

United Nations Framework Convention on Climate Change.

Volgy, Thomas J., and Lawrence E. Imwalle. 1995. "Hegemonic and Bipolar Perspectives on the New World Order." *American Journal of Political Science* 39 (4): 819–34.

Volodin, Andrey. 2017. "The Geopolitics of Crisscrossing Russia–India Investments." *World Affairs: The Journal of International Issues* 21 (3): 120–35.

Walt, Stephen M. 1985. "Alliance Formation and the Balance of World Power." *International Security* 9 (4): 3–43.

Waltz, Kenneth. 1979. *Theory of International Politics.* Reading, MA: Addison-Wesley.

Waltz, Kenneth. N. 2010. *Theory of International Politics.* Long Grove, IL: Waveland Press.

Wasserman, Stanley, and Katherine Faust. 1994. *Social Network Analysis: Methods and Applications.* Cambridge: Cambridge University Press.

White House. 2010. *National Security Strategy.* May. https://obamawhitehouse.archives .gov/sites/default/files/rss_viewer/national_security_strategy.pdf

White House. 2017. *National Security Strategy of the United States of America.* December 18.

Willerton, John P., Gary Goertz, and Michael O. Slobodchikoff. 2015. "Mistrust and Hegemony: Regional Institutional Design, the FSU-CIS, and Russia." *International Area Studies Review* 18 (1): 26–52.

Willerton, John P., Michael O. Slobodchikoff, and Gary Goertz. 2012. "Treaty Networks, Nesting, and Interstate Cooperation: Russia, the FSU, and the CIS." *International Area Studies Review* 15 (1): 59–82.

Wohlforth, William C. 1994. "Realism and the End of the Cold War." *International Security* 19 (3): 91–129.

Wülbers, Shazia Aziz. 2010. *The Paradox of EU-India Relations: Missed Opportunities in Politics, Economics, Development Cooperation, and Culture.* Lanham, MD: Lexington Books.

Yoshimatsu, Hidetaka. 2019. "The Indo-Pacific in Japan's Strategy towards India." *Contemporary Politics* 25 (4): 438–56.

Index

Baker, James, 29
bipolar system, 3, 15, 17–21, 25, 27, 30,
36, 52, 65–66, 113, 117, 140, 151
Brazil, 35, 54–55, 128, 143
BRICS, 35, 54–55, 116, 127–28, 133,
143
Bush, George W., 31–32, 34, 42, 55, 66,
70, 84, 131, 141
Bush, H. W., 29
Bush doctrine, 31, 141

China (People's Republic of), 4–5, 8–10,
16, 31, 33–37, 50, 53–58, 60–61,
67–73, 80–81, 83, 87, 91, 94, 98–
103, 108–10, 116–19, 127–38, 140,
143–51
Churchill, Winston, 23–26
Clinton, William J., 66, 141
Cold War, 3–5, 16, 18, 20–21, 26, 29–31,
34, 36, 49, 52, 55, 65–66, 68, 70, 82–
83, 99, 101–2, 113–15, 131–32, 140–
41, 143

European Union (EU), 10, 41, 47, 50, 54,
56–59, 60, 82–88, 91–93, 96–97, 118,
128, 141–42, 144–48

First World, 5, 68
France, 4–5, 10, 33, 57, 59, 61, 69, 82–83,
85, 92–97, 115, 116, 145–48
Free and Open Indo Pacific Strategy, 9, 71

Germany, 4, 10, 15–16, 23–24, 26,
29–30, 33, 57, 59, 60, 82–83, 85–86,
95–97, 113, 128, 145–48
Great Britain (United Kingdom), 4–5,
10, 15–16, 23–24, 32, 40, 57, 59, 61,
69, 82–84, 87–92, 115, 134, 145–48
global anarchy, 3, 12–13, 38
global order, 3–5, 9, 11–13, 15–25, 31–
37, 45, 51–57, 59–61, 66–67, 69, 83,
97, 99–100, 117, 126–28, 130–31,
134, 138, 141, 143–46, 148, 150–51
Gorbachev, Mikhail Sergeevich, 27–30,
129

hegemon, 3–4, 9, 12–21, 24–27, 30–32,
34, 36–37, 39, 41–42, 45, 51, 53–55,
57, 59, 82, 97, 100, 102–3, 108–9,
118, 128–29, 131–33, 138–39
Hegemonic stability theory, 3, 12–13,
19–20

Iran, 31, 37, 57, 60–61, 68, 73
iron curtain, 25–26

Japan, 9–10, 15, 23, 35, 57, 59, 71, 79,
98–110, 114, 130, 133–35, 145–48

Kashmir, 7–8, 52, 115
Kennan, George, 25–26
Korea, PRK (North Korea), 16, 31, 54,
99, 103, 128

long telegram, 25–26

Modi, Narendra, 55, 56, 101, 115, 117, 125, 129, 133
multipolar system, 7, 16, 18, 21, 33–34, 37, 53–56, 61, 67, 108, 126, 128–32, 134, 138–39, 144–45, 151

NATO, 26, 29–30, 32–33, 36, 44, 53–54, 66–68, 82–83, 114, 128, 140
Nehru, Pandit Jawaharlal, 5–7, 34, 56, 86, 101, 131
Non-aligned Movement (NAM), 5–7, 68
nuclear energy, 89, 93–94, 102, 106–9, 124–26, 146
nuclear weapons, 7, 8, 17, 32, 52, 54, 68, 70, 99, 101, 102, 107, 113–16, 128

Obama, Barack, 34, 53, 55–56, 66–67, 70, 81, 103, 129, 131
One Belt One Road (OBOR), 54, 144

Pakistan, 7–8, 27, 31, 51–52, 65–66, 68, 70, 114–16, 119, 132–34
Power Transition theory, 4, 20
Putin, Vladimir, 31, 53–54, 114, 125, 141

Quad (the), 9, 35, 71, 133

Russian Federation (Russia), 4–5, 8, 10, 23, 30–37, 47, 50–51, 53–58, 60–61, 68–69, 79, 81, 101, 103, 114–32, 135, 137–38, 140–51

Scientific Cooperation, 75–76, 85, 125
Second World, 5, 68
Shanghai Cooperation Organization (SCO), 8, 35, 55, 116, 130, 138, 143–44
South Africa, 35, 47, 49, 54–55, 128, 143
Soviet Union, 3, 5–6, 10, 16, 20, 23–30, 32, 39, 45–46, 52, 54, 65–66, 68, 70, 82, 99, 101, 113–15, 129, 132, 140–41, 144

space (exploration and cooperation), 74–77, 85–86, 92–93, 95, 104, 108, 114, 120–24, 126

terrorism/counterterrorism, 31–32, 35, 68, 73–74, 80, 88, 90–91, 107, 121, 124, 132, 134
Third World, 6, 68
treaties, 9, 32, 35, 37, 41–48, 50–51, 68–69, 72–75, 77–80, 82–83, 86–89, 91–97, 103–6, 108–9, 114–15, 119–25, 134–37, 142; loadstone treaties, 47, 74–75, 89, 91, 105, 109, 119, 121, 136–37
treaty nesting, 35, 43–46, 50–51, 57, 69, 78, 95, 119–21
treaty networks, 35, 37, 50–51, 57, 81, 114
Trump, Donald, 41, 56, 67–68, 70, 103, 129, 134, 139, 144

Ukraine, 33, 54, 115, 128, 138, 141–44
unipolar system, 3, 15, 18–21, 30, 33–34, 37, 49, 52–56, 66, 71, 128–30, 132, 138–40, 144, 151
United Nations, 24, 33, 56, 73–74, 88, 90, 107, 124, 127, 130–31, 133
United States, 3–6, 9–10, 15–16, 18–20, 23–27, 29–37, 41–42, 49, 52–61, 65–72, 74–84, 97–103, 110, 113–20, 127–35, 137–38, 140–51

Vietnam, 16, 26, 113

World War II, 3–4, 16, 20–26, 29, 36, 45, 52, 65, 82, 85–86, 99, 101, 103, 113, 140

Xi Jinping, 133

Yalta agreement, 23–24
Yeltsin, Boris, 140–41

Printed and bound by CPI Group (UK) Ltd, Croydon, CR0 4YY

09/06/2025

14686102-0002